CO[OK ON] A
SH[OE]ESTRING

COOK ON A SHOESTRING

Easy, inspiring recipes on a budget

SOPHIE WRIGHT

photography by Jemma Watts

KYLE BOOKS

First published in Great Britain in 2012 by
Kyle Books
an imprint of Kyle Cathie Limited
23, Howland Street
London W1T 4AY
general.enquiries@kylebooks.com
www.kylebooks.com

ISBN: 978 0 85783 111 8

A CIP catalogue record for this title is available from the British Library

Text © Sophie Wright 2012
Photographs © Jemma Watts 2012
Design © Kyle Books 2012

Editor: Vicky Orchard
Design: Laura Woussen
Photography: Jemma Watts
Food styling: Sophie Wright
Styling: Pippa Jameson
Copy editor: Salima Hirani
Production: Nic Jones and Gemma John

Colour reproduction by ALTA London
Printed ... Offset Printing Co.,

Contents

Introduction

Let's get back to basics. We all know the horrible truth about how over-indulgent and gluttonous we are. All over the world, millions of tons of perfectly edible food is being wasted and thrown away every week. We're all guilty of it, myself included. Over-shopping and buying things we don't really need or have any use for. We have all been seduced by one too many buy-one-get-one-free (BOGOF) deals, the free part of which we usually don't need, so it sits in the bottom of the fridge, or in the fruit basket going bad, until about week later we decide to throw it away. Don't get me wrong, I know the thought was always there, 'I'll do something with that tomorrow', 'I'll blend that into my smoothie at the weekend...' But, inevitably, that poor old brown banana gets thrown out with all the others.

Cook on a Shoestring is a book about waste not want not, about how to train yourself to be a little more economical in these tough times, and not to take the fact that food is so readily available for granted. I know it's easy just to pop to the shops and pick up something for dinner or order a takeaway. Even if we have a few bits in the fridge, those things can often look uninspiring, especially if they have been staring at you for a few days.

My mission is to help you get more for your money. With these easy, tasty and interesting recipes I know I can help to inspire you to use up all those ingredients that might otherwise just be thrown out with the rubbish. Cooking on a budget isn't just about scraping meat off the bones and trying desperately to make another meal out of a chicken carcass, although there will be a bit of that – everyone should have a chicken soup in their repertoire. It's about cooking cleverly, buying wisely and using what you have.

This book is about buying a cut of meat that you might not normally buy because you're not sure how to cook it or what to do with it and utilising it to make more than one tasty, healthy and wholesome dinner. It's also about what do with those soft, slightly squishy tomatoes and limp courgettes that we all will have hanging around at the bottom of our fridges from time to time. It's about buying sensibly, seasonally and economically.

Cooking prime cuts of meat may save you time on a weeknight when you've had a long day at work and just want a quick meal, but they certainly won't save you money. A fantastic braised shoulder of lamb can last for up to four days in the fridge and can be used for a whole host of wonderful main meals, not all of which have to be eaten the same week, so you can freeze your leftovers for an instant dinner at a later date.

I'm going to give you recipes for a whole host of easily obtained cuts of meat. They may have gone out of fashion slightly, but I promise they will save you money and taste just as good, if not better, than prime cuts. Let's revive them. I've included a recipe for pretty much every vegetable that you and I will buy on a weekly basis, but are perhaps slightly uninspiring, down to that last lonely pepper that got overlooked night after night.

I'm not a pretentious cook when it comes to using ingredients that cut corners. Life is busy – if you want to use lazy garlic, or canned apricots just because you have them in the cupboard and don't want to go shopping again, go right ahead. You'll find a tip on nearly every page of this book, helping you to make each meal as easily, cheaply and quickly as possible plus directions as to what recipes you can make with any leftover ingredients you might have.

Finally, as this book is about cooking a little more sensibly and keeping costs down, I will not insist on you going out and buying a thousand different spices and ingredients that you'll only use once. If we use harissa in one recipe, I promise to give you a way of using it again. Right, let's get to work...

My Kitchen Cupboard

I have deliberately used the same spices, oils, mustard and vinegars throughout the book so you don't need to go out and stock up every time you want to cook a new recipe. This list should help you on your way, so stock up gradually when you can. Nothing listed is expensive or difficult to buy.

☆ Flaked sea salt
☆ A pepper mill
☆ Spices: ground cumin, ground coriander, ground ginger, Chinese five spice, ground cinnamon, ground paprika (smoked and hot are both good)
☆ Chilli flakes
☆ Cajun seasoning
☆ Dried oregano or mixed herbs
☆ Stock cubes – chicken and vegetable
☆ Olive oil
☆ Vegetable or sunflower oil
☆ Balsamic/red wine/cider vinegar
☆ Cooking wine
☆ Dijon mustard
☆ Tomato purée
☆ Soy sauce – I like light but either is fine
☆ Worcestershire sauce
☆ Sweet chilli sauce – great for cooking and dipping
☆ Dried grains and pulses: Bulgar wheat, couscous, pearl barley, red lentils – you don't need all of these as they are interchangeable but try to keep a few in stock
☆ Canned pulses: chickpeas, cannellini beans, kidney, flageolet or black beans,

lentils – you don't need all of these as they are all interchangeable but keep a few in stock at all times
☆ Canned sweetcorn
☆ Canned chopped tomatoes/passata
☆ Rice, any variety you prefer. I like wild, Arborio risotto and basmati
☆ Pasta
☆ Dried noodles
☆ Breadcrumbs, dried or fresh
☆ Canned fruits: apricots, peaches and pineapple – these are good to have if you can't get hold of fresh, or if fresh are out of season or expensive
☆ Dried fruits, nuts and seeds: apricots, sultanas, almonds, pine nuts, sunflower seeds – just a couple will do
☆ Flour
☆ Baking powder
☆ Ground almonds
☆ Sugar – brown or white
☆ Icing sugar
☆ Peanut butter
☆ Chocolate spread
☆ Jam
☆ Honey
☆ Vanilla paste or extract – a little goes a long way

IN MY FRIDGE

☆ Butter
☆ Parmesan, Cheddar, mozzarella, ricotta, cream cheese – not all at the same time necessarily
☆ Tomato ketchup
☆ Onions/spring onions/shallots
☆ Chillies
☆ Garlic (pre-chopped or fresh)
☆ Ginger
☆ Milk
☆ Eggs
☆ Cream/crème fraîche/soured cream
☆ Selection of green and root vegetables always including: carrots, celery, leeks, potatoes
☆ Chorizo, smoked bacon, lardons or pepperoni

IN MY FRUIT BOWL

☆ Lemons
☆ Limes
☆ Oranges
☆ Apples/pears (usually interchangeable in recipes)

ON MY WINDOWSILL

☆ Rosemary
☆ Basil
☆ Thyme
☆ Bay
☆ Mint

Meat and Poultry

Meat and Poultry

This chapter contains everything from large cuts of meat to forgotten, old-fashioned favourites and everyday sausage and mince. These recipes show how to replace a very expensive cut of meat with a far more reasonable alternative, how to cook it for the best results and how to make the most of anything you have left.

When buying meat the most important thing to bear in mind is the cooking method. If you buy a cut of meat that is cheaper per kilo this generally means that it will be tougher and need to be cooked for longer for it to become mouthwateringly tender. These type of cuts such as beef brisket, lamb shoulder, or pork belly, are usually larger than more expensive cuts and perfect for a family weekend lunch, but you can also throw them in a low oven or slow cooker to cook while you're at work, or even overnight.

The cooked meat (that cost half the price of more traditional cuts like leg of lamb, sirloin of beef or pork loin) will often be large enough to provide leftovers and these can be used to make a whole host of other delicious recipes. Make the Classic Slow-roasted Shoulder of Lamb with Garden Herbs and Garlic (see page 25) and any uneaten meat can be used for pilafs such as Spiced Lamb and Aubergine Pilaf (see page 33), put in a Lamb, Mint and Potato Pie (see page 30) or made into a nourishing Pearl Barley and Braised Lamb Soup (see page 29). A Spanish-style Roast Chicken with Smoked Paprika, Black Olives and Red Peppers (see page 48) can provide the cooked meat for Bang Bang Chicken Salad (see page 58), Shredded Chicken Quesadillas with Caramelised Onion, Peppers and Chilli (see page 60) or a spicy Chicken, Spinach and Lentil Coconut Curry (see page 65), making your initial meat purchase stretch further and become a real bargain. Throughout the chapter tips provide ideas for what to do with any leftovers and ensure that even if it's just making a stock with a chicken carcass then nothing goes to waste.

Not all the recipes in this chapter require you to cook a large joint of meat, roast a chicken or use up leftovers, some give a taste of what you can cook instead of an unadventurous, and increasingly expensive, chicken breast, with turkey and sausages providing a tasty, cheaper alternative. Turkey is an often overlooked meat and a less expensive variation on chicken, but if you do want to buy chicken then thighs and wings provide great flavour for less money than breasts. Buying sausages rather than larger cuts of meat works well when cooking on a budget and you don't need very many to add flavour to the recipe – try the hearty Sausage and Bean Cobbler (see page 38) or the Rustic Sausage and Tuscan Bean Soup (see page 40).

Meat and poultry are some of the most expensive ingredients and people often think they are unaffordable when cooking on a shoestring. But if you buy the right cuts or the right meat and make the most of what you buy then you can save on cost without having to sacrifice on flavour.

Barbecue Slow-cooked Beef

This great recipe goes a long way when cooking for the family or when entertaining on a budget. Long, slow cooking is the key to making the meal first class, and it really is worth the wait. If you're lucky enough to have good weather, it's taken to a completely different level by finishing it off on the barbecue. This way you can cook the meat in advance and when guests arrive, chargrill for 10–15 minutes for that unforgettable smoky flavour that only barbecuing can give.

Preparation 10 minutes
Cooking 4–5 hours
Serves 6 with leftovers to try
Chilli Beef Ramen on page 22

2kg beef brisket
2 x portions of Barbecue Sauce (see page 172)
2 large onions
100ml water

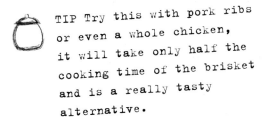

TIP Try this with pork ribs or even a whole chicken, it will take only half the cooking time of the brisket and is a really tasty alternative.

1 Preheat the oven to 130 –140ºC/Gas ½–1. Trim off the really fatty layer on the beef brisket. This can be melted down and used to cook roast potatoes or Yorkshire puddings later if you wish.

2 Coat the beef well in the barbecue sauce, reserving half for basting later. Cut the onions in half, put them in the middle of a solid roasting tin cut-side down and put the beef on top. Add the water to the bottom of the roasting tin to stop the sugar in the sauce burning onto the tin. Cover tightly with kitchen foil, put into the low oven and cook for about 4 hours. Check on the beef every hour or so if possible, basting it with a little more barbecue sauce each time.

3 When you are happy that the brisket is really tender, remove the foil. If you are going to barbecue the beef, now is the time to do it, see instructions below, alternatively increase the heat to 200ºC/Gas 6 to crisp up the outside. Cook for a further 20 minutes before serving. If you intend to finish off the meat on the barbecue, coat the beef well in the leftover sauce and put onto a hot barbecue (ensure the coals are white hot so it doesn't flame too much). Cook for 10–15 minutes until slightly charred and crispy.

4 Serve the beef by carving into thick slices or simply shredding the meat with a fork. This is perfect in big floured baps, with the leftover sauce on the side, or with some coleslaw and barbecued corn.

Pepperpot Beef with Kidney Beans

My mum used to cook this for me all the time, as it was one of my favourites when I was a little girl. For this dish you can use pretty much any cheap cut of beef: brisket, chuck, shin or just braising steak. The fact that it has loads of kidney beans means you can get away with buying less meat if you're on a bit of a tight budget and, served with a jacket potato, it makes a fantastic lunch the next day.

Preparation 15 minutes
Cooking 1½ hours in the oven,
8 hours in a slow cooker
Serves 6

1 tablespoon vegetable oil

700g diced beef, shin, brisket, chuck or braising steak

3 tablespoons plain flour

1 red onion, finely sliced

2 garlic cloves, sliced

100ml water or beef stock

2 teaspoons ground ginger

1 teaspoon chilli powder or paprika

salt and freshly ground black pepper

2 red peppers, deseeded and sliced

3 tablespoons Worcestershire sauce

1 tablespoon brown sugar (or any sugar)

2 tablespoons sweet chilli sauce

1 x 400g can chopped tomatoes

1 x 400g can kidney beans, rinsed and drained (200g if you are using dried beans, soaked overnight and cooked in clean water until tender)

2 tablespoons red wine vinegar (white wine or cider vinegar will also work)

1 Preheat the oven to 160°C/Gas 3, if oven cooking. Put a heavy-based flameproof casserole on the hob and add the oil. While the oil is heating up over a high heat, put the diced beef into a bowl with the flour and coat it well. Gently lay the meat into the hot oil and fry it in batches until all the meat is golden brown, about 4 minutes per side. If cooking in batches, remove the first batch before doing the next one.

2 Turn the heat down to medium, return the meat back to the casserole and add the onion and garlic. Cook for 10 minutes. Coat the onion in the juices in the casserole and add the water or beef stock. Scrape the bottom of the casserole as the water boils to release some of that lovely flavour from sealing the meat. Now add the ginger and chilli powder or paprika, season with salt and pepper, then add the peppers, Worcestershire sauce, brown sugar, sweet chilli, chopped tomatoes, kidney beans and vinegar. Bring the stew to the boil, put on a lid and cook in the preheated oven for 1½ hours. (You can also cook it on the top of the hob over a very low heat for the same length of time.) The beef should be seriously tender when the stew is ready and the sauce will be thick and sticky in consistency.

3 Serve with rice, mashed potato or a crispy-skinned jacket potato.

TIP If you have a slow cooker, simply throw everything in and leave it to cook. It will be perfectly tender by the time you return from work. This also makes a brilliant vegetarian dish, simply substitute the beef for another can of pulses — chickpeas or butter beans work well.

Onglet Steak with Sweet Shallots and Crispy Potatoes

I have this dish every time I go to Paris. We sit outside, drink *vin du table* and watch the world go by. Brasserie steak, onglet or hanger — whatever you want to call it — is a brilliant alternative to over-rated, pricy sirloin, with a much better flavour. Onglet or hanger steak is cut from the skirt of the beef, which is a cut generally used for stewing. However, with some good butchery skills, you can get 5–6 good onglet steaks from one beast. Once cut against the grain, it makes an otherwise tough cut tender and perfect for frying quickly. It's cheap and should have a place on every household's menu at least once a month.

Preparation 15 minutes
Cooking 30 minutes
Serves 4

600g waxy potatoes, peeled and sliced into 4–5mm slices

4 tablespoons olive oil

2 sprigs of thyme, leaves only

4 garlic cloves, chopped

salt and freshly ground black pepper

4 shallots, finely sliced

4 onglet steaks, weighing about 200g each (if you can't get these, bavette is similar and the same price)

1 Preheat the oven to 200°C/Gas 6. Put the sliced potatoes on a non-stick baking tray (you may need two) and drizzle with 2 tablespoons olive oil, half the thyme leaves and half the chopped garlic. Season with salt and pepper and toss everything together well. Ensure the potatoes don't overlap too much as this could result in uneven cooking. Cook in the preheated oven for 25 minutes. Check the potatoes halfway through the cooking time – you may need to move the ones from the edges of the tray in towards the centre, and the ones from the middle to the outside.

2 While the potatoes are cooking you can make the sweet shallots. Put 1 tablespoon of olive oil in a frying pan and add the shallots along with the remaining garlic and thyme. Season with salt and pepper and leave to cook over a low heat for 20 minutes or so. You want them to be soft but not coloured.

3 When the shallots and potatoes are nearly cooked, heat another frying pan and add the remaining oil. Season the steaks well with salt and pepper and when the pan is really hot lay them into the oil. Cook for 4 minutes on each side for medium steaks. Ensure the pan is really hot so the steaks are nicely caramelised, as this will really add to the flavour of the final dish. Once cooked, leave them to rest while you serve up the potatoes.

4 Stir any juices from the rested steak into the shallots. Serve the steak with the potatoes and top with the shallots and some roasted baby vine tomatoes if you like. Dijon mustard is essential – oh, and a glass of red wine.

Cola-braised Sticky Beef Short Ribs

Juicy, sticky and gelatinous: beef short ribs are my new favourite cut. Please don't think I'm crazy cooking meat in Coca-Cola — the sugar helps the meat caramelise perfectly and the acidity balances the flavours. This is a seriously inexpensive dish and you get lots for your money. The ribs take a little while to cook, but who cares? The preparation is so easy, and you can leave the ribs in the oven while you get on and do whatever it is that needs doing. I promise it's worth the wait.

Preparation 15 minutes
Cooking 2–2½ hours
Serves 6

330ml regular Coca-Cola (this matters, diet Coca-Cola will not work in the same way)
2 teaspoons Chinese five-spice powder
2 tablespoons tomato purée
5cm piece of fresh ginger, peeled and grated
75ml vinegar (cider, red wine or white wine)
1 teaspoon chilli flakes
100ml sweet chilli sauce
2kg short ribs, cut through the bone about 8–10cm long and excess fat trimmed

1 Preheat the oven to 160ºC/Gas 3. Put all the ingredients except the ribs in a saucepan and bring to the boil. Simmer for 8–10 minutes before taking the pan off the heat.

2 Put the ribs into a deep-sided solid baking tray or a large casserole and pour over three-quarters of the marinade. Coat the ribs well in the sauce, then cover the tray in foil or with a tight-fitting lid. Cook in the preheated oven for 1 hour.

3 After an hour, check on the ribs, turn them over and ensure the marinade isn't burning. Brush the ribs with the remaining sauce and add a little water if the pan is drying out (it will burn slightly around the edges because of the amount of sugar in the sauce). Replace the foil and cook for another hour until the meat is falling from the bones.

4 If you want to crisp up the ribs slightly, remove the foil and increase the oven temperature to 200ºC/Gas 6. Cook for about 15 minutes until they have caramelised on top.

5 Serve the ribs with a buttery jacket potato and a large green salad.

Pot Roast Brisket with Onions and a Super-quick French Onion Soup

Brisket is a bit of a forgotten cut in the world of cookery books. It's very well priced and easily obtainable if you live near a good high-street butcher or supermarket with a specialist meat counter. Cooking really doesn't get much simpler than this.

Preparation 5 minutes
Cooking 4–4½ hours
Serves 8, plus a soup and scraps
for sandwiches

2–2.5kg brisket
salt and freshly ground black pepper
4 tablespoons vegetable oil
4 large onions, sliced
2 tablespoons plain flour
4 tablespoons Worcestershire sauce
2 litres beef stock (cube or concentrate is fine,
if you don't have homemade)
2 sprigs of thyme and rosemary
2 bay leaves

1 Preheat the oven to 140°C/Gas 1. If the brisket has a layer of fat on the top side, score this using a sharp knife and season generously with salt and pepper.

2 Put a large flameproof casserole on the hob and set the heat to high. Add the oil and lay in the meat joint on the fat side. Cook for 6–8 minutes on each side. Once coloured all over, remove the meat from the casserole and set aside.

3 Put the onions into the casserole. Stir them in the meat juices, then put on the lid and cook over a low heat for 10–15 minutes.

4 Once the onions are soft, add the flour. Coat the onions well before returning the beef back to the casserole. Now add the Worcestershire sauce, beef stock and herbs. Bring to the boil, cover tightly with kitchen foil to trap in all the steam and juices, put the lid on top and transfer to the oven. Cook for 3½–4 hours.

5. Once the beef is tender, remove it from the casserole and allow to rest. Reserve the stock and onions for making French Onion Soup (see below). Carve the meat into thick slices and serve with boiled potatoes and English mustard.

French Onion Soup with Cheesy Croutons

Once you have cooked the meat in all those lovely meat juices, allow the stock to cool completely, then chill in the fridge overnight. The following day, remove the layer of fat that will have formed on the top of the liquor. (Keep this for cooking roast potatoes in next week.) Put the stock and onions back on the hob and give it a taste to check for seasoning. Toast a few pieces of stale bread under the grill (one or two per person) before smothering in the cheese of your choice and a dash or two of Worcestershire sauce. Grill until the cheese has completely melted and is seriously bubbling. Serve the soup with lots of the onions add a cheesy crouton to each bowl and a sprinkling of parsley if you have some – an almost free meal!

Chilli Beef Ramen

We should all have a Ramen in our repertoire. It takes only minutes to whip up and can be made on a very tight budget. Adapt this recipe as you wish. I have made it with both raw and cooked beef and both are equally good. This is a wonderful dish to make for one, if you don't particularly fancy cooking or need a meal in a hurry without having to visit the shops.

Preparation 10 minutes
Cooking 10 minutes
Serves 2

1 litre beef stock (chicken and vegetable will also work fine)
2.5cm piece of fresh ginger, peeled and grated
2 red chillies, thinly sliced
2 tablespoons light soy sauce
100g noodles of your choice (I recommend egg, udon or glass noodles)
300g beef, cooked and shredded or raw, thinly sliced (use skirt or frying steak)
50g bean sprouts
50g baby leaf or big leaf spinach
3 spring onions

To serve
a few sprigs of fresh coriander
2 lime wedges

1 Pour the stock into a saucepan, put it over a low heat and add the ginger, chillies and soy sauce. Bring to the boil.

2 Add the noodles and cook according to the packet instructions – 4–6 minutes will usually do the trick.

3 Now add the beef and cook for 2–3 minutes. If you're using raw beef, cook it gently until it is just cooked and still slightly rare.

4 Finally, add the bean sprouts, spinach and spring onions. Heat through until the spinach has wilted before serving in large bowls, garnished with coriander sprigs and with a lime wedge to squeeze over, if you wish.

Lamb Samosas

Samosas are brilliant finger food, perfect for a starter, a picnic or a quick lunch on the go. You can make these in batches and freeze them after wrapping, then cook them from frozen as and when you need them. They are very cheap to make and offer a brilliant way of using up leftovers.

Preparation 25 minutes
Cooking 10–20 minutes
Makes 12

250g cooked shredded lamb or lamb mince

50g cooked potatoes, diced into 1cm pieces

50g cooked peas

2 tablespoons lime pickle

2cm piece of fresh ginger, peeled and grated

1 garlic clove, grated

1 teaspoon ground cumin

¼ teaspoon hot chilli powder

salt and freshly ground black pepper

6 filo pastry sheets or 3 samosa wrappers

4 tablespoons vegetable oil, for cooking

lime wedges

mango chutney

1 Put the lamb, potatoes, peas, lime pickle, ginger, garlic and spices into a bowl and mix well. Season with salt and pepper.

2 Lay out three sheets of filo pastry, brush them with water and then lay another sheet on top of each one to make a double layer. Take the doubled filo sheets and cut each into four 10cm strips. Spoon 1 tablespoon of the filling onto the bottom corner of each strip. Brush with a little water to ensure the pastry will stick in place. Fold the corner of the part of the pastry on which the filling is sitting over on the diagonal to enclose the filling. Continue folding on the diagonal along each strip to create a sealed triangular parcel – you'll get about 4–5 folds out of each pastry strip. Brush with a little of the oil and set aside until you are ready to cook them. These can also be frozen at this stage.

3 Pour all of the remaining oil into a frying pan. When hot, gently lay in the samosas and cook for 2–3 minutes per side until golden brown. These can also be baked in a preheated oven at 200°C/Gas 6 for 15 minutes.

4 Serve with a wedge of lime and some mango chutney on the side.

> TIP These samosas are a perfect way to use up any bits from the Slow Roasted Shoulder of Lamb on page 25. They are also fantastic with any vegetables you have in the fridge. as well as pork or chicken.

TIP When cooking the lamb shoulder this way, make sure you buy it with the bone in so you can make the Pearl Barley and Braised Lamb soup tomorrow — see page 29 for the recipe.

Classic Slow-roasted Shoulder of Lamb with Garden Herbs and Garlic

Cooking a shoulder of lamb doesn't get more straightforward than this. This recipe works on exactly the same principle as roasting a leg, only you cook it for longer. Shoulder of lamb is far cheaper to buy than leg and if I were being totally honest, I would say that shoulder is a far superior cut of meat. The flavour from all the fat gives the meat an unbelievable richness and keeps it moist during cooking. The meat will fall off the bone in lovely big chunks and the top layer of fat will be perfectly crisp and golden brown. If you buy a big enough shoulder, you can shred up any meat that's left over the next day to throw together a number of dishes.

Preparation 10 minutes
Cooking 4½–5 hours
Serves 4 with leftovers, 6 without

8 large sprigs of rosemary
6–8 bay leaves
1 head of garlic, cut in half across the equator
1 shoulder of lamb, bone in, weighing about 2–2.5kg
4 tablespoons olive oil
salt and freshly ground black pepper

1 Preheat the oven to 200°C/Gas 6. Lay the rosemary and bay leaves on the bottom of a deep roasting tin along with the garlic. Ensure the garlic is put cut-side up so that it can soak up all the lamb juices while it cooks.

2 Take the shoulder of lamb and score the fat with a sharp knife about 5 or 6 times – this will help the fat to render and melt while the lamb cooks and will keep the meat nice and moist. Rub the shoulder all over with the oil and season. Lay the lamb on top of the herbs, fatty-side up. Wrap the tin tightly in kitchen foil and put in the preheated oven. As soon as the lamb is in, turn the oven down to 160°C/Gas 3 and leave to cook for 4½–5 hours. If you can, check the lamb once or twice. If you think it's over-colouring in any way, simply turn the temperature down. The lamb is cooked when it is falling apart – you shouldn't even need a knife to carve it.

3 Serve with braised flageolet beans and curly kale.

TIP Get your rosemary from the garden if you can or picked out of the windowbox and save yourself a few pennies. Don't worry if the sprigs are a bit weathered or woody, they'll still taste great. Remember to give them a little wash if you have pussycats lurking in your garden!

Lamb Shoulder Shank Tagine

Hands up, I confess — it's the fault of us chefs that the once very reasonable lamb shank has rocketed in price. It still tastes the same as it did five years ago, but supply and demand has doubled the price of this fantastically versatile and flavoursome cut. Well, I'm here to the rescue with a little chef's secret. I want to introduce you to the shoulder shank: it's slightly smaller than a leg shank and can be cooked in exactly the same way, and here's the best part: it's half the price. If you can't get hold of lamb shoulder shank try some portioned scrag end, it's very cheap and cooks down to become incredibly tender. You want to use a cut of meat that has a bone in it for extra flavour.

Preparation 15 minutes
Cooking 3½ hours
Serves 4 (with leftover sauce for another dish)

4 tablespoons vegetable oil
4 lamb shoulder shanks (leg shank, scrag end or even a whole shoulder will also do a great job)
2 onions, sliced
2 garlic cloves, sliced
2.5cm piece fresh ginger, peeled and grated or 2 teaspoons ground ginger
3 teaspoons ground cumin
1 cinnamon stick or ¼ teaspoon ground cinnamon
pinch of dried chilli flakes (optional)
2 tablespoons tomato purée
150g dates or dried apricots, halved and pitted
salt and freshly ground black pepper
1 litre lamb stock (chicken or veg stock will do as well, and cubes are fine)
1 x 400g can chopped tomatoes
coriander leaves, to garnish

1 Put a large flameproof casserole on the hob over a high heat and add half the vegetable oil. Once the casserole is hot, lay in the lamb shoulder shanks and seal on each side until golden brown — about 4 minutes per side. Once the lamb is sealed and well coloured (remember — colour equals flavour), remove it from the casserole and set aside.

2 Reduce the heat and add the rest of the oil along with the onions. Please feel free to add any diced veggies that you may have to use up: carrot, celery, leek or even peppers will work really well. Put the lid on and allow the onions to cook for 4–5 minutes before removing the lid, adding the sliced garlic, ginger, cumin and cinnamon. Add the chilli at this stage as well, if using. (If you have some Harissa from page 172 you can use this here in place of the garlic, spices and chilli.) Coat the onions well in the spices before adding the tomato purée and dried dates or apricots. Put the lamb back into the pan. Season well with salt and pepper.

3 Add the stock and the canned tomatoes. Bring the tagine to the boil, reduce the heat, put the lid back on top and leave to cook for 3 hours. You want the meat to be falling off the bone. This can also be cooked in a really low oven at about 140°C/Gas 1 for the same amount of time.

4 Scatter over some coriander leaves and serve the tagine with the Moroccan Carrot and Chickpeas on page 105 or with Sweet Potato and Bulgar Wheat Salad with Pomegranate (see page 108) or just as it is with some green beans on the side.

TIP If you have any sauce
left over after your meal,
don't throw it away. Make the
Moroccan Carrot and Chickpeas
on page 105 and fold through.

Stuffed and Rolled Shoulder of Moroccan Spiced Lamb

This is a great dinner party-recipe that you can make without spending lots on expensive ingredients. It calls for bits that most people have in their storecupboards, such as spices and dried apricots, as these things don't go off. I often find that when I cook a new recipe, I am left with a little, or sometimes a lot, of ingredients that I will never use again. Well, I hope I can help you to use them up now.

Preparation 30 minutes
Cooking 3–3½ hours
Serves 4 comfortably with leftovers,
6 without

1 boned shoulder of lamb, weighing about
1 –1.25kg (boned weight)
2 teaspoons ground cumin
2 teaspoons ground coriander
2 teaspoons dried oregano or mixed herbs
2 garlic cloves, grated
3 tablespoons olive oil

For the stuffing
2 tablespoons olive oil
30g butter
1 onion, chopped
2 teaspoons ground cumin
2 teaspoons ground coriander
2 teaspoons dried oregano or mixed herbs
200g ready-to-eat apricots, chopped
125g fresh breadcrumbs
salt and freshly ground black pepper
1 large egg

1 Preheat the oven to 150°C/Gas 2. To make the stuffing, set a frying pan over a medium heat and add the olive oil and butter, then the chopped onion, and cook for 5–6 minutes until the onion is tender. Add the cumin, coriander and dried herbs and cook for a further 2–3 minutes. Keep the onion moving around in the pan so that it doesn't burn.

2 Transfer the cooked onion and spices into a food processor along with the apricots and blitz to a chunky paste. Add the breadcrumbs, season and blitz again before adding the egg. Make sure the mixture is well combined and set aside to cool.

3 Once the stuffing has cooled you can stuff, roll and tie the lamb. Put the boned shoulder on a board with the flesh-side facing up and the fat-side directly on the board. Spoon the stuffing mixture along the middle of the shoulder. Now roll the shoulder tightly around the stuffing. Take 4–5 pieces of kitchen string and tie the now-rolled shoulder tightly in place.

4 Combine the cumin, coriander, oregano or dried herbs, garlic and olive oil in a small dish and season. Rub this mixture over the tied and rolled lamb. Put the lamb into a roasting tin. Cover tightly with kitchen foil and cook in the preheated oven for 3 hours. (You can speed up the cooking time by 1½ hours by simply turning the oven to 180°C/Gas 4, but I find the meat is never as tender if I do this.)

5 Once the lamb has had about 3 hours, remove it from the oven and leave to rest. Carve it in thick slices and serve with some natural yogurt mixed with a couple of spoonfuls of Harissa (see page 172), if you wish.

Pearl Barley and Braised Lamb Soup

This soup is ideal for using up any leftovers from a delicious Classic Slow-roasted Shoulder of Lamb (see page 25) from Sunday lunch. You need very little meat to make this dish tasty, as you can use the bone from the shoulder of lamb to really pack this simple soup full of flavour. You can use just about any vegetables to bulk out this soup, so it's a great way of utilising any leftovers or forgotten veggies hanging about in the bottom of your fridge.

Preparation 15 minutes
Cooking 1¼ hours
Serves 4–6

2 tablespoons olive oil

1 large onion, sliced

salt and freshly ground black pepper

300g cooked lamb, shredded, plus the bone

raw lamb neck fillet, diced, will also work if you are starting from scratch)

2 bay leaves

1.5 litres stock (lamb, beef or chicken)

75g pearl barley

600g root vegetables such as carrot, parsnip, turnip, swede, potatoes, squash, peeled and diced into 2.5cm pieces

To serve

2 tablespoons freshly chopped parsley leaves

crusty bread and butter

1 Put a large flameproof casserole on the hob and add the olive oil. Add the onion and a pinch of salt, put on the lid and cook over a low heat for 15 minutes. Stir every 5 minutes to prevent burning. Increase the heat and add the cooked lamb or diced raw neck fillet and the lamb bone. Add the bay leaves and stock and simmer gently for 30 minutes. Skim off any impurities that come to the surface using a ladle while the broth is cooking.

2 After 30 minutes, add the pearl barley and all the vegetables. Season with salt and pepper and cook for 15 minutes until the vegetables are all cooked. Check for seasoning and remove the lamb bone.

3 Serve the soup with lots of freshly chopped parsley and a big hunk of crusty bread and butter.

Lamb, Mint and Potato Pie

A fantastic way to use up the extra meat from a roast shoulder of lamb.

Preparation 20 minutes, plus chilling
Cooking 1¼ –1½ hours, plus cooling
Serves 4–6

For the pastry

450g plain flour, plus extra for dusting
150g cold lard (or butter for a richer pastry),
cubed, plus extra for greasing
1 large egg
½ teaspoon salt
2 tablespoons milk or water, if needed
1 large egg beaten with a pinch of salt
(eggwash)

For the filling

2 tablespoons vegetable oil
1 large onion, finely diced
1 large leek, finely sliced
450g cooked lamb, shredded (you can also
use minced lamb if you don't have time to
braise the lamb first)
450g boiled diced potatoes, carrot and swede
(or any other root veg you may have in your
fridge)
2 tablespoons mint sauce
salt and freshly ground black pepper

To serve

Homemade Pickled Vegetables (see page 136)
chutney

1 Preheat the oven to 180°C/Gas 4. Sift the flour into a large bowl and add the cubes of lard. Using your fingertips, rub the fat into the flour until the mixture resembles breadcrumbs. Add one egg and the salt. If the mixture still looks a bit dry, add the milk or water. Gently knead the mixture until it has a smooth texture, then wrap it in clingfilm and leave to rest in the fridge for 30 minutes.

2 Put a frying pan on the hob and add the vegetable oil. Fry the onion and leek over a low heat for 5–6 minutes until soft before adding the shredded lamb, cooked root vegetables, mint sauce and some salt and pepper. Simmer for 10 minutes. Leave to cool.

3 Remove the pastry from the fridge. Cut off a quarter, wrap it in clingfilm and set aside for the pie lid. Grease a 25 x 10cm loaf tin with a little lard or butter. Roll out the pastry to about 3mm thick on a well-floured surface. Gently lay the rolled pastry into the loaf tin. Press it into all the corners of the tin, ensuring the whole dish is covered. Leave the edges of the pastry overhanging the rim. Put the lined pastry case in the fridge for another 15 minutes to rest.

4 Cut a piece of greaseproof paper and lay it into the lined pastry case. Fill with baking beans and bake for 20 minutes. Remove the beans and brush the inside of the pastry case with the eggwash and bake for another 5–10 minutes.

5 Pour the cooled lamb mixture into the baked pastry case. Roll out the final piece of pastry for the lid. Cut off four thin strips of the raw pastry and brush the edges of the pastry case with the eggwash. Press the strips onto the edges of the tin to seal the lid in place. Brush with eggwash again and lay the lid on top. Press the edges down using your fingers or a fork to make sure you get a well-sealed edge. Trim off any excess raw or cooked pastry from around the edges using a small sharp knife. Brush the top with the remaining eggwash and make a small hole in the centre to let the steam escape. Sprinkle with sea salt and put the pie on a baking tray and into the oven for 35 minutes or until golden brown on top. Allow to cool before slicing and serving with pickles and chutney.

TIP If you want to make this
recipe and don't have any
leftover shoulder of lamb, try
slow braising 3-4 lamb neck
fillets for a few hours before
shredding the meat to use for
the pie.

Lamb and Tomato Hotpot

This type of dish is perfect for a quick weekend lunch or an easy-to-prepare weeknight dinner. Not many ingredients are involved, so there's not much mucking about with chopping and, best of all, it is all cooked in one pot, so there's little need for much washing up.

Preparation 20 minutes
Cooking 1½ hours
Serves 4–6

2 tablespoons vegetable oil
4–6 large lamb neck chops on the bone or
800g lamb neck fillet, if you prefer
2 tablespoons flour
salt and freshly ground black pepper
3 large onions, sliced
1 bay leaf
600g potatoes, peeled and sliced
into 0.25cm slices
400g tomatoes, sliced
1 tablespoon Worcestershire Sauce
500ml chicken or lamb stock
50g butter

1 Preheat the oven to 180°C/Gas 4. Put a large flameproof casserole on the hob and add the vegetable oil. Set the heat to high.

2 Dust the lamb with flour and season with salt and pepper before gently laying it into the hot oil and browning on all sides – this should take about 4–5 minutes. You may need to do this in batches depending on the size of the casserole. Transfer the lamb to a plate once browned and set aside.

3 Clean out any burnt bits from the bottom of the pan and add the sliced onions. Add a pinch of salt and the bay leaf and cook for 6–8 minutes over a low heat until the onions are soft and sweet. Now remove the onions and put on the plate next to the lamb.

4 Take the casserole off the hob and put into it a layer of the sliced potatoes. Season with salt and pepper, then add a layer of sliced tomatoes, then a spoonful of the onions, followed by the sealed lamb. Now add another layer of tomatoes, then the onions and, finally, finish with potatoes.

5 Mix the Worcestershire sauce with the stock and pour this over the hotpot. Dot with the butter, season with salt and pepper and cover with a lid or with kitchen foil. Put the casserole in the preheated oven and cook for 1 hour, then remove the foil and cook for another 30 minutes.

6 Serve straight away with a large chunk of crusty bread.

Spiced Lamb and Aubergine Pilaf

If you have taken my advice from the introduction and have a reasonably stocked spice cupboard (cumin, cinnamon, chilli, coriander), you can make this dish with hardly any fuss and on a very modest budget. Aubergines are like little sponges and will soak up whatever flavours you throw at them. They are great to pair with lamb because they soak up all the lovely fat, leaving you with loads of flavour but none of the grease. I make this dish on a weeknight as a quick and easy supper, or to roll into wraps at the peak of a successful party, when everyone is feeling a little light-headed from one too many drinks and needs a little pick-me-up — it works every time.

Preparation 5 minutes
Cooking 1½ hours
Serves 6 as a main course or
8 for wraps or a light lunch

2–3 medium aubergines, cut into 2cm pieces

3 tablespoons olive oil

salt and freshly ground black pepper

1 large onion, diced

2 garlic cloves, chopped

500g lamb mince

2 teaspoons ground cumin

½ teaspoon ground cinnamon

2 teaspoons ground coriander

1 teaspoon ground turmeric

75g sultanas, chopped dried apricots, or dates

200g chopped tomatoes, fresh or canned

250g white rice (I like basmati, but any will do)

600ml lamb or chicken stock

75g toasted pine nuts or flaked almonds (optional)

10–15 fresh mint leaves, shredded (optional)

To serve (optional)

natural or Greek yogurt

8 flatbreads

1 Preheat the oven to 180°C/Gas 4. Put the prepared aubergine onto a baking tray (you may need two), drizzle with 2 tablespoons of the olive oil and season. Bake in the preheated oven for 25 minutes, turning once halfway through. Ensure the aubergine pieces on the edges of the tray don't burn.

2 While the aubergine is cooking, put a large flameproof casserole on the hob and add the remaining oil. Once the oil is hot, add the onion and garlic, then season and cook for 10 minutes over a low heat until the onion is soft and translucent.

3 Now add the lamb, increase the heat and seal for 5 minutes. You want the lamb mince to have a little colour. Add the spices, the cooked aubergine, the sultanas and the chopped tomatoes and stir well. Cook for 8–10 minutes to allow the spices to cook. Season again.

4 Add the rice. Coat it well in all the spices and pan juices before adding the stock. Put on the lid and bring to the boil, then transfer the casserole to the oven and cook for 35–40 minutes. Check it once whilst cooking – if it looks like it needs a little more stock, now is a good time to add it.

5 You may want to add some toasted nuts and freshly shredded mint before taking the dish to the table. I love to have this with griddled flatbreads and some Greek yogurt.

Slow-cooked Roasted Pork Belly with Apples

Slow-cooked pork belly is the ultimate comfort food for me. The longer you can leave it in the oven, the better. You simply can't overcook this dish, providing the oven is at the right temperature. This recipe presents possibly the simplest way of preparing pork belly, and the great thing is that you should have plenty left over to make another dish the next day. The same rules apply to this recipe as to many of the others in the book: buy a little more than you need for one meal so leftovers can be used up over the week.

Preparation 15 minutes
Cooking 4 hours
Serves 6 with leftovers

2kg boneless pork belly
sea salt
2 large onions, cut horizontally into
2–3 thick slices
350ml chicken stock, cider or apple juice
2 Bramley apples (but any apple will do), cut
horizontally into 3–4 thick slices

1 Preheat the oven to 140°C/Gas 1. Score the skin of the pork using a sharp knife. Pat the skin dry with kitchen paper and rub flaked salt into the skin.

2 Take a large roasting tin and lay the sliced onions in the middle. These will act as a trivet for the pork to sit on. Sit the pork on top of the onions and cover with kitchen foil. Pour over 250ml of the stock or juice and cook in the oven for 3 hours.

3 After 3 hours, take the pork from the oven and remove the foil. Increase the heat to 200°C/Gas 6. Tuck the apples under the pork belly with the onions, pour in the remaining 100ml of stock or juice and put the dish back into the oven for another 45 minutes–1 hour to allow the skin to crisp up.

4 Remove the pork from the oven and allow to rest for 15 minutes before carving into chunky slices and serving with the apples.

TIP The onions will be lovely and sweet, so they are perfect for serving with the pork belly dish. Alternatively, save them to mix with some mashed potatoes, mould into patties and pan-fry for 3 minutes per side for a potato cake that's perfect with a poached egg and some wilted spinach.

Pulled Pork Spring Rolls

This is a useful recipe to make with leftovers from Chinese Five-spice Pork Stew (see page 36). The spring rolls can also be made with leftover chicken, minced pork or simply kept veggie, so no one will miss out!

Preparation 20 minutes
Cooking 10 minutes
Makes 8

400g cooked pork, shredded (cooked chicken
or raw minced pork will do, see Tip)
2 carrots, peeled and finely grated
50g bean sprouts
2.5cm piece of fresh ginger, peeled and grated
1 garlic clove, grated
30g freshly chopped coriander
2 tablespoons sweet chilli sauce, plus extra
for dipping, or cooking juices from
the pork dish on page 36
juice of 1 lime
8 sheets of filo pastry or
12cm spring roll wrappers
200ml vegetable oil, for frying,
plus extra for brushing

1 In a bowl, mix the shredded pork, carrots, bean sprouts, ginger, garlic, coriander, sweet chilli or cooking juices and lime juice.

2 If using filo pastry, cut each sheet in half. Brush one half with a little oil and lay the other half over the top. If using spring roll wrappers, you don't need to do this. Spoon a tablespoon of the pork mixture into the centre of each wrapper. Fold in each end and roll up the spring roll. Use a little water to secure the wrappers in place.

3 Heat the oil in a deep saucepan or wok. Check it is hot enough by dropping in a little piece of bread. If it turns golden brown instantly, the oil is ready. Carefully lower the spring rolls into the hot oil and cook for about 3 minutes until golden brown. Remove from the oil using tongs or a slotted spoon and put onto a plate lined with kitchen paper to remove the excess oil. Serve while hot with some sweet chilli or the plum sauce to dip.

TIP You can use raw pork mince to create this recipe, follow the above instructions, just cook at 180°C and for 5–6 minutes to give the meat time to cook.

Chinese Five-spice Pork Stew

I once cooked this dish for a dinner party and it was a huge hit. The problem is that, for ages, I've been racking my brains trying to remember how it did it! I have been experimenting and I think I have just about mastered it again. Brilliant with sticky rice and perhaps a few stir-fried veggies, this pork dish can be thrown together on the cheap and I promise it will feel like you've just eaten in a five-star Chinese restaurant.

Preparation 15 minutes
Cooking 3½–4 hours
Serves 6

2 tablespoons vegetable oil
2kg pork shoulder, diced
3 teaspoons Chinese five-spice powder
or 1½ teaspoons ground ginger, ½ teaspoon
ground cinnamon, 1½ teaspoons
ground coriander
2 star anise (optional)
½ teaspoon chilli flakes or 1 large red chilli,
chopped
2 garlic cloves, chopped
2.cm piece of fresh ginger, peeled and grated
3 tablespoons tomato purée
3 tablespoons brown sugar
1.5 litres chicken or vegetable stock
125ml dark soy sauce
3 peppers, colour of your choice,
cut into 2.5cm pieces

To serve
1 red chilli, sliced
4 spring onions, sliced
sticky rice

1 Preheat the oven to 130°C/Gas ½. Heat the oil in a large flameproof casserole set over a high heat. Add the pork and seal for 5–6 minutes before adding the Chinese five-spice powder or spices, star anise, if using, chilli flakes, garlic and ginger. Cook the spices with the pork for a few minutes before adding the tomato purée, brown sugar, stock and the soy sauce. Bring to the boil, put on the lid and cook in the oven for 3 hours. Check that the stew isn't drying out as it cooks. If necessary, add a little more stock.

2 After 3 hours, add the peppers and cook for another 30 minutes. Once the pork is tender and falling apart, remove the casserole from the oven, sprinkle the stew with sliced red chilli and spring onions and serve with sticky rice.

TIP This dish tastes better the next day! Eat just as it is or rolled into Pulled Pork Spring Rolls (page 35) and served with sweet chilli sauce.

Sausage and Bean Cobbler

A cobbler is an American dish that is usually sweet, but I personally prefer it savoury. It's much like a savoury scone or dumpling soaked in lovely rich tomato sauce — what can possibly not be good about that?

Preparation 10 minutes
Cooking 1 hour
Serves 4–6

1 tablespoon olive oil
4 sausages, removed from skins
1 large onion, diced
2 garlic cloves, chopped
2 celery sticks, chopped
pinch of chilli flakes
1 tablespoon tomato purée
1 x 400g can butter beans, rinsed and drained
1 x 400g can cannellini beans, rinsed and drained
2 x 400g cans chopped tomatoes
(or 600ml passata)

For the topping
225g self-raising flour
90g cold butter, cubed
175ml milk
2 teaspoons dried oregano
salt and freshly ground black pepper

1 Preheat the oven to 200°C/Gas 6. Put a sauté pan on the hob and add the oil, then the sausagemeat. Break the meat up with a wooden spoon or spatula before adding the onion, garlic, celery and chilli flakes. Cook, covered, over a low heat for 6–7 minutes.

2 Add the tomato purée, the beans and chopped tomatoes or passata. Bring to the boil and simmer for 20 minutes while you make the cobbler topping.

3 Place the flour in a clean bowl. Add the cubes of butter and rub them into the flour using your fingers until the mixture resembles breadcrumbs. Now add the milk and the dried oregano. Season with salt and pepper and mix until you have a firm, smooth dough.

4 Spoon the sausage and bean mixture into a baking dish. Tear off small golf-ball sized pieces of the cobbler dough and sit them on top of the sausage stew. You can have a few gaps and it's nice if some bits stick upwards as these will become lovely and golden as it cooks. Cook in the preheated oven for 25–30 minutes or until the top is golden brown.

5 Serve with a large salad.

Rustic Tuscan Bean and Sausage Soup

Turn to this recipe when it's cold outside, you don't particularly fancy venturing out and you need something warm and comforting in your belly. This soup is brilliant for adults and children at any time of the day. It contains lots of carbs to keep you going, and the best part is that it's even better the next day, so make a little extra!

Preparation 10 minutes
Cooking 30–40 minutes
Serves 4

2 tablespoons olive oil
2–3 pork sausages, removed from skins (try to use a sausage with a little extra flavour)
1 large onion, finely chopped
2 garlic cloves, chopped
2 celery sticks, diced
1 carrot, peeled and diced
3 tablespoons tomato purée
1 litre chicken or vegetable stock
400g can haricot or cannellini beans, rinsed and drained
salt and freshly ground black pepper

Optional
green cabbage such as kale or Savoy, cut into large strips
tomatoes that have seen better days, chopped
courgette, chopped

To serve
crusty bread
Parmesan cheese, grated

1 Put a large flameproof casserole or pan on the hob and add the olive oil along with the sausagemeat, breaking it up roughly with your fingers. Brown the sausagemeat for a few minutes and break it up a little more with a spatula.

2 Add the onion, garlic, celery and carrot and cook for a further 5–6 minutes. Add the tomato purée, the stock and the beans. Season and simmer for 20–30 minutes.

3 If you are adding any cabbage, tomatoes or courgettes to the soup, add them 5 minutes before serving so that they don't overcook. Serve with crusty bread and a little Parmesan, if you wish.

TIP This dish can be made using dried haricot or cannellini beans instead of cooked canned beans. Soak 200g dried beans overnight in cold water, then boil them in fresh water for 1 hour or until tender.

TIP Make one extra and freeze it. It's always useful to have something ready-made just in case.

Pork Parmigiana

I often cook this dish if I'm trying to have a carb-free week. It's great as a vegetarian option, without the meat. I often layer it with mozzarella, which is the classic version of a parmigiana, or roll it with ricotta and spinach —a kind of twist on cannelloni. This version is an enchilada-meets-a-parmigiana and I love it. It also reheats really well in the microwave so it's perfect for a work lunch or a quick dinner before rushing out again.

Preparation 20 minutes
Cooking 45 minutes
Serves 4

2–3 large aubergines, cut into thin strips
lengthways
2 tablespoons olive oil
salt and freshly ground black pepper
500g pork mince (you can also use turkey
mince for this recipe)
2 garlic cloves, grated
2 teaspoons dried oregano
pinch of nutmeg
zest of 1 lemon
1 bunch (15 leaves) fresh basil
1 x 125–150g mozzarella ball, torn into strips
25g grated Parmesan

For the tomato sauce
2 tablespoons olive oil
2 garlic cloves, chopped
500ml passata or 2 x 400g cans chopped
tomatoes
½ teaspoon chilli flakes

1 Preheat the oven to 200°C /Gas 6. Heat a frying pan or griddle on the highest setting. Put the aubergine slices into a bowl and add the olive oil. Season with salt and pepper. Lay the aubergine slices in the pan (don't overcrowd it – you can do this in batches). Cook until looking lovely and golden brown underneath, about 3–4 minutes, turn them over and cook the other sides. Remove from the pan and leave to cool.

2 Next, put the pork mince into a bowl and add the garlic, oregano, nutmeg, lemon zest and salt and pepper. Mix well.

3 To make the sauce, combine all the sauce ingredients in a saucepan and simmer for 10 minutes. If you are using canned tomatoes you may want to blend the sauce to make it smooth, but it's up to you.

4 Now lay out the fried aubergine slices. Put a spoonful of the pork mince at one end of each slice, lay a basil leaf on top along with a piece of mozzarella and roll the aubergine up tightly. Spoon some of the hot tomato sauce into the base of a baking dish. Arrange the aubergine rolls in the dish and cover with the remaining sauce. Add any remaining mozzarella or basil leaves. Sprinkle generously with grated Parmesan and bake in the hot oven for 35–40 minutes.

5 Remove from the oven once golden brown and serve.

Potato, Ham and Cheese Bake

I'm a simple girl really. I don't like things overly complicated, I like them for a good price and to be easy to prepare – like this recipe. You could serve this as a meal on its own with just a salad or some boiled peas on the side.

**Preparation 20 minutes
Cooking 1 hour
Serves 6–8**

25g butter
1 tablespoon vegetable oil
1 large onion, diced
250g cooked ham, cut into 1cm pieces
2 tablespoons chopped parsley, fresh or
frozen is fine (optional)
salt and freshly ground black pepper
1.5kg potatoes (waxy ones are best), peeled
250ml double cream
2 garlic cloves, sliced
100g grated cheese, Cheddar, Red Leicester,
mozzarella or Monterey Jack

1 Preheat the oven to 180°C/Gas 4. Put a frying pan on the hob and add the butter and oil. Add the onion and cook for 5–6 minutes until sweet and translucent. Now add the diced ham and the chopped parsley, if using. Season with pepper and remove from the hob.

2 Slice the potatoes to about 2-3mm thick. If you have a mandolin, use this.

3 Put the cream and sliced garlic into a saucepan and bring to just below boiling point. Season with salt and pepper. Butter a 30 x 20cm baking dish. Pour 2–3 tablespoons of the cream mix into the bottom. Arrange a layer of the sliced potatoes over the bottom of the dish, followed by a couple of tablespoons of the onion, ham and parsley mix, then a couple of tablespoons of grated cheese. Season with pepper before adding another layer of potatoes, more cream and more onion, ham and parsley, then cheese. Continue until you have used up all the ingredients. Finish with a layer of potatoes and cover with grated cheese. Cover with kitchen foil and put in the preheated oven for 25 minutes before removing the foil and cooking for another 30 minutes.

4 Serve straight from the oven to the table.

TIP Make sure you save some back for yourself for tomorrow's lunch.

The Classic Roast Chicken
with Lemon, Rosemary and Garlic

Roasting a chicken can be a tricky business. Getting maximum flavour and beautifully moist meat is a skill that few have mastered. It's not hard to get it wrong and end up with a tough and sometimes slightly dry old bird. Success is all down to cooking temperatures, timings, the all-important basting and, of course, not being scared of not cooking the chicken thoroughly enough. So here's how I do mine. It's not a clever and intricate recipe, it's simply my favourite Sunday lunch, which also gives me plenty of meat to make another delicious meal for the following day.

Preparation 10 minutes
Cooking 2 hours 10 minutes
Serves 4 for dinner, with plenty left over for recipes on pages 58–65

1 whole chicken, weighing 2.25kg
75g butter
1 lemon
1 head of garlic
2 sprigs of rosemary leaves, chopped
salt and freshly ground black pepper
1 tablespoon olive oil

1 Preheat the oven to 200°C/Gas 6. If the chicken has its giblets inside, remove these and leave to one side. (You can make a fantastic gravy or stock with these later, see page 174.)

2 To flavour the chicken, cut the butter into 5–6 pieces and put in a small bowl. Grate the zest of the lemon into the butter. Peel one garlic clove and, using the same grater, grate it into the butter as well. Add the chopped rosemary, a large pinch of salt and a good twist of black pepper. Using a wooden spoon or your hands, squish all the ingredients together until the butter is soft and everything is well incorporated.

3 To prepare the chicken, put it in a deep roasting tin. Cut away the sting that has trussed the bird. (I do this so that the chicken can cook more evenly – leaving the legs tied so close to the breast will slow down the cooking time and could leave you with dry breast meat and undercooked legs. The finished roasted bird won't look quite as picture-perfect as some, but it will be perfectly cooked.) Rub the butter all over the skin of the bird. I sometimes put the butter under the skin as well for a really intense flavour. If you want to do this, gently release the skin on the breast using your fingers and push the flavoured butter between the skin and flesh. Be careful not to tear the skin. Cut the already zested lemon in half and put it into the cavity of the chicken. Release all the garlic cloves from the bulb, leaving the skins on, and put these inside the cavity along with a good pinch of salt and pepper. Season inside the bird as well as out, as this will really bring out the flavour in the meat and the gravy. Finally, drizzle with the olive oil.

4 Put in the oven and increase the temperature to 220°C/Gas 7 for the first 10 minutes of cooking – the outside of the chicken will start to become lovely and crispy and golden brown. Then reduce the temperature to 190°C/Gas 5 and cook for about 15 minutes per 450g plus an extra 10 minutes cooking time – so for 1 hour 35–40 minutes for the weight suggested in this recipe. While the chicken is cooking, you must remember to baste it: every 20–30 minutes open the oven door, carefully tilt the roasting tin towards you and, using a baster or tablespoon, spoon the juices in the tin over the top of the chicken. This will give you a very moist chicken as well as a perfectly golden brown, crispy skin.

5 Once you are happy that the chicken is cooked – you can check this by seeing if the leg pulls away easily from the carcass and that the juices run clear – remove from the oven and leave to rest. This is the most important part. If you don't rest the chicken it will be dry – I rest mine for at least 10 minutes.

6 To carve the chicken, pull each leg away from the carcass. When you can see where the leg joins the body, use the knife to release it completely. It is joined by a ball and socket joint so you shouldn't have to cut through any bone at all. Divide the legs into two thighs and two drumsticks. Again, these are joined by a ball and socket so it should make easy work. Remove the wings in exactly the same way. These can be a little more fiddly and may break apart, as they will be more cooked than the rest of the bird, but don't worry about that. You are now left with just the crown. Cut along the backbone and pull each breast away from the carcass. If the chicken is cooked well this will happen very easily. When you reach the wishbone, just cut around it, trying to remove as much of the flesh as you can. Cut the breast into 5–6 thick slices and serve with a piece of the leg and some gravy (see page 174).

TIPS Try to always have garlic in your kitchen; it will make a plain meal come to life. Don't be scared of overdoing it with the garlic either. If you roast the garlic cloves in their skins, after roasting you will be left with the sweetest flesh that will have soaked up lots of those wonderful chicken juices and add the perfect finish to an otherwise slightly unexciting gravy.
Rosemary grows best in pots so a patio plant or one on the windowsill is perfect and will save you pennies in the long run.

Spanish-style Roast Chicken with Smoked Paprika, Black Olives and Red Peppers

This smoky, garlicky roast chicken doesn't have to be for a Sunday lunch and makes a brilliant midweek supper. It's packed with flavour, and whatever is left can be used for a whole host of other things, from a cheeky twist on paella to salads, omelettes or even tomato-based soups.

Preparation 20 minutes
Cooking 1 hour 50 minutes
Serves 4, with enough for another meal tomorrow, or 6 for a really big meal today

50g butter
2 teaspoons smoked paprika
zest of 2 lemons
1 teaspoon dried oregano
2 garlic cloves, peeled and grated
salt and freshly ground black pepper
1 whole chicken, weighing 2.25kg
1 tablespoon olive oil

For the roasted vegetables
2 red peppers, cut into 5cm pieces
2 red onions, cut into wedges
2 tablespoons pitted black olives
500g baby new potatoes
125g cherry tomatoes
1 teaspoon smoked paprika
1 teaspoon dried oregano
1 tablespoon olive oil

1 Preheat the oven to 220°C/Gas 7. Cut the butter into small pieces and put in a bowl. Add the paprika, lemon zest, oregano and garlic and squish all the ingredients together until the butter is soft and everything is well incorporated. Season the butter with salt and pepper. Rub the butter all over the skin of the chicken and under the skin if you wish (see page 46 for instructions).

2 Remove the string or elastic from the chicken and put it in a deep roasting tin. (Don't forget to check for giblets! If you have some, the recipe on page 174 explains how to use them.) Drizzle the chicken with the olive oil and put in the preheated oven for 10 minutes before turning the oven down to 190°C/Gas 5. Remember to baste the chicken with the butter, some of which will have melted into the baking tray, every 20–30 minutes.

3 To make the roasted vegetables place all the vegetables in a large bowl and coat well in the paprika, oregano, salt and pepper and the olive oil.

4 Once the chicken has cooked for 40 minutes, take it out of the oven and scatter the veggies around the outside. This will be a good time to baste the bird again and coat all the vegetables in the juices. Put the tray back into the oven and cook for the remaining 45 minutes. If the vegetables look as though they are over-colouring, put a sheet of kitchen foil over the baking tray for the final 20 minutes of cooking.

5 When the time is up, check that everything is cooked perfectly before removing the chicken from the roasting tin and leaving it to rest for at least 10 minutes. Keep the vegetables warm in a low oven. Carve as instructed on page 47 and serve with the vegetables and all the lovely cooking juices.

One-pot Chicken

The simplicity of this dish is what makes it so special. The French name is *pot-au-feu*, which translates as 'pot on the fire', which is exactly what you do. You take a whole chicken, put it in a pot, put the pot on the fire and let it cook — for as long as it needs. Then add very simple, unpretentious vegetables and you've got a dinner, and almost definitely a lunch, and without a doubt a fantastic broth, so nothing from that plump bird goes to waste.

Preparation 15 minutes
Cooking 1½ hours
Serves 4, with plenty left for later

1 whole chicken, weighing 2–2.5kg

2 chicken stock cubes

1 bouquet garni (2 sprigs of thyme, 2 bay leaves, 2 sprigs of rosemary bundled together in the green of a leek leaf and tied with string)

salt

2 leeks, white parts only, cut into 5cm pieces

3 large carrots, peeled and cut into 5cm pieces

1 white onion, peeled and cut into wedges

3 celery sticks, peeled and cut into 7.5cm pieces

125g pearl barley or 8–10 small peeled waxy potatoes, such as Charlotte (optional)

white pepper

To serve

25g freshly chopped flatleaf parsley leaves

crusty bread

1 Put the chicken in a large soup pan with a tight-fitting lid and cover completely with water. Put the pan on the hob and bring to the boil. Once boiling, add the stock cubes, bouquet garni and a pinch of salt and allow to simmer over a low heat for 40 minutes. While the chicken is cooking, if you notice any white froth or 'scum' rising to the top, simply skim it off using a ladle or large spoon.

2 Add the leeks, carrots, onion and celery to the pan. Add a little more water, if needed, and cook for another 40–45 minutes. If you want to bulk out this dish, add the pearl barley or potatoes.

3 Once all the vegetables are cooked, turn off the heat. Taste the broth to ensure that you are happy with the flavour. Add a little more seasoning of you feel it needs it. I prefer to use white pepper in this dish, but it's your call.

4 Using two large spoons or a carving fork, remove the chicken from the broth. Put it in a dish and allow it to cool until you can shred it by hand. A fresh pair of rubber or latex gloves will help protect your hands from the heat if you are in a bit of a hurry or impatient like me. Shred the leg and wing meat into the bottom of warmed bowls. If you want to use the breast meat as well, do so; if not, save it for tomorrow (to use in one of the other delicious cooked chicken recipes on the following pages). Dish out a generous amount of vegetables and the broth on top of the chicken and serve with chopped parsley and a big chunk of crusty bread.

Go Asian

If you're in the mood for something a little more exotic, try making the broth with a hint of the Orient. Add a couple of spilt red chillies, a smashed stick of lemongrass, a 2.5cm peeled chunk of ginger and a splash of soy sauce and fish sauce. Replace the vegetables with some Far Eastern vegetables, such as pak choi, bean sprouts, mangetout, baby sweetcorn and Chinese cabbage, and cook until tender. Add glass noodles at the end of cooking instead of pearl barley or potatoes to bulk out the dish a bit.

WHAT TO DO NOW?
If you have leftover broth, remove and drain the vegetables and freeze the broth. The next time you make a risotto or some gravy for Sunday lunch, it will be there ready and waiting to be used as stock. I love a freebie!

Blitz any leftover vegetables to a smooth vegetable soup, add a can of tomatoes for a bit of extra bulk and a splash of cream or a spoonful of crème fraîche. Store in the freezer for a cold day.

As for leftover chicken...flick through pages 58-65 for a bit of inspiration.

TIP The method in this recipe is one that can be used for almost any cheap cut of meat. The very classic French version uses ham hock, shin of beef and smoked sausage. This makes a wonderful meal, which is extremely cheap to produce and will feed you and quite possibly the neighbours for a whole week!

Mum's Midweek Honey and Lemon Chicken

A weeknight staple when I was a little girl, this dish was probably also one of the first things I ever cooked on my own. I make mine using chicken thighs — I prefer the taste to breast and they cost half the price. I buy them with the skin on, so I can get them nice and crispy in the oven. Serve this dish with boiled rice and green beans.

Preparation 5 minutes
Cooking 25 minutes
Serves 4

2 tablespoons runny honey
3 garlic cloves, grated
juice of 2 lemons
1 heaped teaspoon wholegrain mustard
1 tablespoon olive oil
salt and freshly ground black pepper
8 chicken thighs, bone in and skin

To serve
boiled rice and green beans

1 Preheat the oven to 190°C/Gas 5. Combine all the ingredients, except the chicken, in a bowl and mix well. Coat the chicken in the mixture and put in a baking dish. Reserve the remaining sauce. Put the dish in the oven and cook for 25 minutes. Halfway through the cooking time, pour over the rest of the sauce. The chicken should be cooked through and the skin will be nice and crispy and golden brown.

2 Serve with rice and green beans and pour over the extra sauce in the bottom of the baking dish. This is also delicious accompanied with the Greek-style Rice Salad (see page 100).

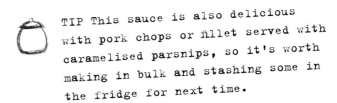

TIP This sauce is also delicious with pork chops or fillet served with caramelised parsnips, so it's worth making in bulk and stashing some in the fridge for next time.

Oven-baked Chicken Jambalaya

I make a variation of this dish once a week at home. It's quick to put together and there is enough of it to take to work for lunch the next day, so there's no need to buy a sandwich.

Preparation 10 minutes
Cooking 45 minutes
Serves 4, with enough for lunch the next day

2 tablespoons olive oil
6–8 chicken thighs, bone in, with skin on
4 teaspoons Cajun seasoning
2 red peppers, deseeded and cut into 1cm pieces
1 large onion, sliced
1 large red chilli, finely chopped
2 garlic cloves, sliced
75–100g chorizo, sliced (optional)
300g long grain rice
500ml hot chicken stock
1 x 400g can chopped tomatoes
salt and freshly ground black pepper
100g green beans, cut into 5cm pieces
100g fresh peas

To serve
1 lemon, cut into wedges
salad

1 Preheat the oven to 180°C/Gas 4. Heat a flameproof casserole over a medium heat and add half the olive oil. Season the chicken thighs with 1 teaspoon of the Cajun seasoning and lay them in the hot oil. Fry for 3–4 minutes per side until the skin starts to turn golden brown. Remove and set aside.

2 Add the remaining olive oil to the casserole and add the peppers, onion, chilli, garlic and chorizo, if using. Cook for 5–7 minutes before adding the remaining Cajun seasoning and the rice. Coat the rice well in all the juices at the bottom of the casserole, then pour in the hot stock and add the canned tomatoes. Stir well and season before covering with a tight-fitting lid and putting the casserole into the oven for 20 minutes.

3 After 15 minutes of cooking time, remove the casserole from the oven and stir well before adding the green beans and peas. Stir again before adding the fried chicken to the top of the rice dish. Put the lid on the casserole, put it in the oven and cook for a further 15 minutes. Check there is enough stock – you can always add a little more if it looks as if it is drying out.

4 Check the rice is cooked before serving with a wedge of lemon and a side salad.

TIP If you have some Jambalaya left over and don't fancy taking it to work for lunch, buy some soured cream, an over-ripe avocado and some soft tortilla wraps on your way home. It will make a fantastic burrito filling.

Thai-style Chicken Wings

I always cook chicken wings for a friendly get-together. Not just because they are seriously easy to cook and make great finger food, but also because they are very cheap and, believe me, if your family or friends have appetites like mine do, the cheaper option is always a good thing as they will get through tons of food! This marinade is not only great with chicken wings, drumsticks and breasts but also fantastic with meaty white fish such as hake, coley, pollock or even some prawns.

Preparation 15 minutes
Cooking 25 minutes
Serves 4 as a dinner

20–25 chicken wings (1kg total weight)

For the marinade
3 tablespoons Thai Green Curry Paste
(see page 173)
2 tablespoons clear honey or sugar

To serve
lime wedges

1 Make the marinade by combining the Thai Green Curry Paste and honey or sugar in a bowl. Put the chicken wings in a bowl and spoon over the marinade then leave to marinate for a few hours or overnight, if you have time. However, this is a strong marinade and you will still get a great flavour if you wish to cook the wings straightaway.

2 Preheat the oven to 220°C/Gas 7. Put the marinated chicken wings onto a non-stick baking tray and bake for 20–25 minutes. Turn the wings halfway through cooking if they look like one side is over-colouring. Remove from the oven and serve with a wedge of lime and a bowl of dipping sauce (see Tip).

TIP If serving as finger food, serve with 2 teaspoons of the marinade, 1 tablespoon of soy sauce and 2 of sweet chilli sauce mixed together as a dip on the side.

Make a batch of this marinade and store it. Add a can of coconut milk with a few frozen prawns and you'll have an instant Thai curry.

Bang Bang Chicken Salad

This quick dish can be made on a tight budget if you have some cooked chicken left over in the fridge from a previous dinner. If you don't, buy yourself some chicken drumsticks and give them 15–20 minutes in the oven at 190°C/Gas 5 to use for this tasty weeknight delight.

Preparation 15 minutes
Cooking 15–30 minutes
Serves 4

½ cucumber, seeds removed and cut into thin strips
1 large carrot, grated
6 spring onions, cut into thin strips
200g glass noodles, cooked according to the packet instructions and refreshed in cold water
300–400g cooked chicken

For the dressing

3 tablespoons crunchy peanut butter
2 tablespoons soy sauce
2 tablespoons sweet chilli sauce
½ teaspoon chilli flakes
juice of 1 lime
3 tablespoons water

To serve

20g fresh coriander, torn
1 tablespoon toasted, crushed peanuts (optional)
1 lime (optional)

1 If you have made the Green Thai Curry Paste (see page 173) or Harissa (see page 172) you can add a little of this to the chicken before you cook it to jazz it up a little. If not, a pinch of chilli and salt and pepper will do the job.

2 Make the dressing for the salad first by combining the peanut butter, soy sauce, sweet chilli sauce, chilli flakes and lime juice together in a small saucepan. Set the pan over a low heat for 4–5 minutes to allow the dressing to warm through. Add the water to loosen the consistency once the sauce is warm.

3 Mix the cucumber, carrot and spring onions with the cooled noodles. Mix well to ensure the ingredients are evenly distributed throughout the salad.

4 Shred the cooked chicken. If you have cooked chicken thighs, simply slice them into 5–6 strips per thigh. Mix the chicken into the salad, then pour over the warm sauce and stir through.

5 Serve in large soup bowls with torn coriander, toasted peanuts and a wedge of lime, if using.

> TIP This dish is lovely cold the next day for lunch if you have any left over.

Shredded Chicken Quesadillas with Caramelised Onion, Peppers and Chilli

This is a new take on a dish from my last book *Home at 7, Dinner at 8* that went down extremely well. It's super quick to make, involves minimal shopping - as most of these ingredients are likely to be found in a well-stocked cupboard and, best of all, it's cheap and cheerful. You'll need some leftover chicken from one of the fabulous roasts on pages 46–50, as this recipe only works with shredded cooked chicken. However, it does also work very well as a veggie option – trying adding some leftover chilli from page 119. Alternatively, tear or snip over some ham if you happen to have some in the fridge.

Preparation 10 minutes
Cooking 25 minutes
Serves 2–3

2 tablespoons olive oil

3 peppers (you choose the colours), thinly sliced

2 red onions, thinly sliced

1 teaspoon chilli flakes

salt

1 teaspoon sherry or red wine vinegar

300g cooked chicken, shredded

4 tortilla wraps

2 tablespoons tomato purée

75g grated cheese (Cheddar, mozzarella or even a goat's cheese log works really well)

1 small bunch coriander (about 35–40g)

To serve (optional)
soured cream
pickled chillies
crispy salad

1 Put a frying pan over a medium heat and add the olive oil. Put the peppers and onions into the pan with the chilli flakes. Cook for 6–8 minutes before adding a pinch of salt and the vinegar. Reduce the heat to low and cook for another 5 minutes until the onions are soft and sweet. Once all the liquid has evaporated, add the shredded chicken and mix well.

2 Next, spread two of the four tortillas with the tomato purée. Put a griddle pan on the hob and set the heat to medium. Put one of the tortillas that is spread with tomato purée into the pan, spread-side up. Lay on half the pepper, chicken and onion mix and spread it out evenly. Add half the cheese and scatter over half the coriander. Put a plain tortilla on top and cook for 3 minutes before turning over and cooking the other side for another 3 minutes. Once you can see that the cheese has melted, remove the cooked quesadilla from the pan and repeat the process with the other pair of tortillas.

3 Serve with a big spoonful of soured cream, a few pickled chillies and a crispy salad if you wish.

> TIP These can also be done in a frying pan if you don't have a griddle pan.

Chicken, Orzo and Minted Pea Broth

Orzo, giant couscous or even macaroni all work for this recipe. Cook this the night after having roast chicken and you can use the bones for a lovely stock. Add a handful or two of frozen petit pois with leftover meat and you'll have yourself a perfectly light and healthy supper that the whole family can enjoy. Frozen herbs will work just as well as fresh.

Preparation 10 minutes
Cooking 15 minutes
Serves 4

750ml chicken stock (see page 174 or a couple of stock cubes will do the trick)
50g orzo pasta
2 garlic cloves, finely sliced
2 celery sticks, finely chopped
100g, cooked roast chicken shredded
100g frozen peas
4 spring onions, finely chopped
30g fresh mint (frozen will also do)

To serve
crusty bread
large mixed salad

1 Pour the chicken stock into a large saucepan and put over a high heat. Once boiling, add the orzo, garlic and celery. Allow this to cook for 10–12 minutes until the pasta is completely cooked.

2 Now add the shredded chicken, peas and spring onions. Heat through before adding the mint.

3 Serve with crusty bread or a large mixed salad.

TIP This soup is the ideal vehicle to use up all your leftover bits and pieces. Everything from roasted parsnips left over from the Sunday roast, to mushrooms from last week's shop that are looking a little the worse for wear. Simply chop everything to roughly the same size, chuck it all into a large saucepan and allow it to simmer.

Chicken, Spinach and Lentil Coconut Curry

You can throw this meal together in a matter of minutes by simply opening a can, engaging in a bit of rough chopping and shredding some leftover chicken. It's also great as a vegetarian option if you happen to have a few aubergines laying about to replace the chicken. This is a real all-rounder kind of a dish and one that can be cooked in one big pot, so a thumbs-up for those of us who have our hands constantly submerged in the depths of the washing-up bowl after dinner. Perfect with steamed rice, this meal can be knocked up within 30 minutes without breaking the bank.

Preparation 10 minutes
Cooking 30 minutes
Serves 4

2 tablespoons vegetable oil
4 tablespoons Indian curry paste
(see page 172)
450–500g cooked chicken (or raw chicken, using boneless and skinned thighs, diced into 2cm pieces)
2 sweet potatoes, peeled and diced into 2cm pieces
120g red split lentils
600ml coconut milk
500ml chicken stock
400g washed baby spinach
juice of 1 lime
40g coriander, roughly chopped
1 green chilli, thinly sliced (optional)

To serve
steamed rice

1 Put a large wok or flameproof casserole on the hob. Add the vegetable oil and allow it to heat up. Add the curry paste and cook for 1 minute or so before adding the raw chicken, and cook for 5 minutes to seal.

2 Add the diced sweet potato and the lentils and coat well in the paste. If you are using cooked chicken, add it now, along with the coconut milk and stock. (You can add the stock from frozen if you have taken it straight from the freezer – just allow an extra 5 minutes' cooking time.) Bring to the boil, then reduce the heat to low and simmer for 20 minutes.

3 Once the sweet potato and lentils are tender, and the curry has thickened, add the spinach and allow it to wilt for 3–4 minutes before removing the pan from the heat. Squeeze in the lime juice and scatter over the coriander and green chilli, if using. Allow the curry to sit for a few minutes off the heat before serving with steamed rice.

TIPS Rather than buy two cans of coconut milk, try buying the smaller cartons so you're not left with any leftovers after making this recipe. Alternatively, blend any leftover coconut milk into a smoothie with a banana and some fresh pineapple as a weekend family treat.

Cajun-style Turkey Burgers

OK, I know what you're all thinking — turkey? Let me assure you that this burger, if made right, with lots of lovely seasoning, is seriously good and very tasty. It's better for you than beef, is much cheaper to prepare, and it is great for the whole family with or without the bun.

Preparation 10 minutes
Cooking 15 minutes
Serves 4

600g turkey mince

1 egg

3 teaspoons Cajun seasoning (if you don't have this, try equal quantities of cumin, paprika and dried herbs)

1 tablespoon Worcestershire sauce

salt and freshly ground black pepper

1 tablespoon vegetable or sunflower oil

To serve

1 ripe avocado

4 burger buns (or grilled bagels)

lettuce

sliced tomato

sliced red onion

griddled corn on the cob (optional)

1 Preheat the oven to 190°C/Gas 5. To make the turkey burgers, mix the turkey mince with the egg, Cajun seasoning, Worcestershire sauce, salt and pepper. I do this with my hands but you can use a spoon if you prefer.

2 Divide the mix into four equal portions and shape into round patties. Make them quite flat as they will rise as they cook. Make a little dip in the middle of each patty so that they are nice and flat by the time they are have cooked. These can now be put into the fridge for cooking later or can be cooked straightaway.

3 Heat a large frying pan and add the oil. When the oil is hot, lay in the patties and cook for 2–3 minutes per side until they are golden brown. Transfer them to a baking tray and put into the oven to cook for a further 8 minutes (they should be cooked all the way through without any pinkness).

4 While the burgers are cooking, mash the avocado with the chermoula, if using, and mix well to make a salsa.

5 Remove the burgers from the oven and allow them to rest while you toast the burger buns. Cut the buns in half horizontally and toast them in the hot oven for a few minutes.

6 To serve the turkey burgers, lay some lettuce and sliced onion on the bottom layer of each toasted bun, followed by a turkey burger. Add some more lettuce, a few slices of tomato and top with the burger bun top. Serve these with Sweet Potato Wedges, if you wish. (To make the wedges cut 3–4 medium sweet potatoes into 8–10 large wedges. Put in a bowl with 2 teaspoons of Cajun seasoning, salt, pepper and 1 tablespoon of vegetable or sunflower oil. Bake on a baking tray at 180°C/Gas 4 for 25–30 minutes, turning halfway through cooking.)

Roast Dinner Turnovers

This is a recipe that can be adapted to use up just about any bits and bobs that you may have not quite managed to finish at the dinner table. My personal favourite version is a Christmas Dinner Turnover, which is basically delicious cold Christmas dinner leftovers packed into a flaky pastry parcel. If you're lucky, you might be the one who gets the pigs in blankets tucked underneath the scrumptious pie filling. This dish can be made with lamb, pork, beef or chicken...even fish. It's perfect for tomorrow's lunchbox or a lunchtime snack on the go.

Preparation 15 minutes
Cooking 25–30 minutes
**Serves...depends on how greedy your guests
are but you should get 2–3 turnovers**

flour, for dusting
500g shortcrust or ready-rolled puff pastry
(shop-bought is fine)
1 egg, beaten
500–600g leftover roast dinner (such as
shredded meat, roast potatoes, carrots, peas,
cauliflower cheese, roast parsnips, stuffing)
sea salt

1 Preheat the oven to 180°C/Gas 4. Dust a clean worksurface with flour and roll out the pastry into a large rectangle that's about 2–3mm thick. Cut the rectangle into 2–3 smaller rectangles (or circles, if you prefer turnovers of a traditional Cornish pasty shape). Ensure they are about the same size. Brush them with a little beaten egg around the edges.

2 Ensure the roast dinner leftovers are completely cold (I often wait until the following day to make this dish). Mix the leftovers together in a large bowl and break up any bits that may be a little on the big side. Spoon the leftovers generously into the middle of each pastry sheet. Now fold the pastry over from one side to the other to make the edges meet and to seal in the filling. Use your fingers to crimp the edges, then trim off any excess pastry. Do this with all of the turnovers. Brush the turnovers with the remaining egg, sprinkle with a little sea salt and put onto a non-stick baking tray or a tray lined with greaseproof paper.

3 Bake in the preheated oven for 25–30 minutes until golden brown.

4 Serve hot or cold with English mustard on the side.

TIP Make up the turnovers and freeze them before they're baked. When you have a nice stash, bake them off and they will be perfect for an outing to the park when summer finally arrives.

Fish

Fish

Cooking with fish and cooking economically, while at the same time living in the middle of London, is often a bit of a struggle. If I lived on the Cornish coast I would definitely be making friends with my local fishermen and I'm sure my wallet would be a lot fuller after my purchasing than it is now after a trip to my local fishmonger.

Fish is one of the most expensive ingredients to cook with and you need to be savvy about which type of fish to buy, especially if you don't have access to a local supply. This chapter gives recipes using the cheapest and most easily accessible fish that are also simple to cook and still deliver on flavour and quality. I hope these will give you enough of an overview about this amazing ingredient that is available to all of us and encourage you to use it in a more economical way.

From my extensive knowledge of supermarkets (I literally spend my whole life in them!) I know you will find most, if not all, of the fish that I am giving you recipes for there. I wouldn't put something in my cookbook that is so obscure you have to travel to the Billingsgate Market at 4am to get your hands on it. We all lead busy lives, so I understand that ingredients need to be readily available. However, if you can't find a certain type of fish, and you are lucky enough to still have a fishmonger on your high street, please ask him or her to get it for you or simply to replace it with a just as good equivalent. I can assure you they will be more than happy to do this.

I find it best to cook fish simply. It loves citrus flavours, especially the more oily fishes, and wonderful fragrant aromatics like ginger, lemongrass and chilli. It's quite surprising the amount of flavours you can add without them totally overpowering your fishy dish, especially when cooking oily and smoked fish (which feature frequently throughout this chapter).

A really important point to remember when cooking any fish is not to overcook it. Whilst the fish is cooking, keep checking it. If it's a flaky fish like pollock it should fall apart in nice firm white chunks when cooked. If it's an oilier fish like salmon or mackerel, don't cook it for so long that all the white proteins start oozing out of the fish and make it almost unpleasant in texture to eat. Give it some love and show it a bit of respect.

A top tip when buying fish is trying not to buy fish already cut into portions, as you pay more for this. If buying salmon for dinner, get the whole fillet. Cut off the pieces you want for that evening's meal and freeze the tail end and any other trimmings you don't need. These, once you have acquired enough, will make a very wholesome dinner. You might not get a whole meal all at once, but if you do this the next week with the some smoked haddock you'll have a nice little stash in the freezer for the Maryland Sweet Potato Fishcakes (see page 82) or the perfect comforting fish pie. Comforting not only because it tastes delicious but also because you've made a meal that cost nearly nothing.

Leek and Smoked Haddock Soup

This hearty soup could just as easily be classed as a stew. Smoked haddock is my preference here, but this dish is also great made with some lightly smoked mackerel or kippers. It's really easy to prepare and uses very few ingredients. The thing about smoked fish is that, because of its bold flavour, a little goes a long way, leaving you with enough change to buy yourself a nice glass of wine or two to go with it.

Preparation 10 minutes
Cooking 20 minutes
Serves 4

20g butter
2 leeks, sliced into rings
400g potatoes, peeled and cut into 1cm dice
salt and freshly ground black pepper
400ml milk
600ml fish, chicken or vegetable stock
400g smoked haddock
1 tablespoon plain flour
1 tablespoon freshly chopped parsley
leaves (optional)

1 Put a medium saucepan or sauté pan on the hob and add the butter. Allow it to melt before adding the leeks and potatoes with a pinch of salt and some pepper. Cook for 10 minutes until the leeks are soft.

2 Meanwhile, pour the milk and the stock into another pan and add the fish. Bring to the boil before removing the fish from the poaching liquor. When cool enough to handle, flake the fish into chunks. Set the cooking liquor aside.

3 Add the flour to the leeks and potatoes and stir well. Cook the flour for a few minutes before adding the hot poaching liquor. Mix well and bring to the boil. Simmer until the potatoes are tender.

4 Add the fish to the soup and taste for seasoning. Stir in the chopped parsley, if using, and serve.

Blackened Fish with Orange and Watercress

Just about any fish works well with this recipe, so I won't tell you which one you buy. Because fish is such a perishable ingredient with a short shelf-life, shopkeepers often run deals and special promotions to help them to sell it all quickly, before it's no longer fit to be sold. So remember this recipe and snap up those bargains next time you're out shopping. Buy yourself an orange and a bag of peppery watercress on your way out and you'll be able to knock up a quick and tasty meal in no time for a fantastic price.

**Preparation 10 minutes,
plus marinating
Cooking 10 minutes
Serves 2**

2 x 130–150g fish fillets (coley, hake, pollock
or salmon work well), skin on or off
1 tablespoon vegetable, olive or sunflower oil
orange zest, to garnish (optional)

For the marinade

4 tablespoons dark soy sauce
2 tablespoons clear honey
1 teaspoon ground ginger
2 teaspoons rice wine vinegar (if you don't
have this you can use balsamic vinegar)
1 teaspoon chilli flakes (optional)

For the salad

1 teaspoon Dijon mustard
1 tablespoon clear honey
1 large orange
salt and freshly ground black pepper
3 tablespoons olive oil
200g watercress

1 If the fish has skin on it, score the skin a few times with a sharp knife to allow the marinade to penetrate, then put the fish in a dish. Now make the marinade. Measure out all the ingredients and pour over the fish. Leave in the fridge to marinate for as long as you can. Overnight is great, but if you only have 10 minutes, that's fine.

2 While the fish is marinating, make the dressing for the salad. Mix the Dijon mustard with the honey and set aside. Segment the orange by cutting off the top and the bottom to create two flat surfaces. Using a small sharp or serrated knife, remove the peel and the white pith from around the orange. Now remove the flesh from the individual segments, but leave the membrane behind. Do this into a bowl and allow the segments to fall into it along with the juice. Once you have finished, squeeze all the juice out of the membrane that is left. Pour the juice into the mustard and honey mixture and stir well before seasoning with salt and pepper and adding the olive oil.

3 Now it's time to cook the fish. Heat the oil in a non-stick frying pan set over a high heat. When hot, lay in the fish, skin-side down, if it has skin on it. Cook for 4–5 minutes before turning the fish, pouring in any remaining marinade and cooking for another 5–6 minutes. You want the fish to go quite dark and the marinade to be quite sticky and reduced. Once you are happy that the fish is cooked, turn off the heat and leave the fish to rest while you finish the salad.

4 Mix the watercress with the orange segments and pour over the dressing. Serve the salad with the fish. Pour any marinade over the fish just before serving, garnished with orange zest, if you wish.

Grilled Sardine Sandwich

This was mine and my mum's carpet picnic treat when I was a little girl. It was a huge deal not to sit at the dinner table, but very, very rarely we would sit on the floor, crossed legged, with our favourite Sunday evening supper. It's not posh, but it's one of my favourite memories.

Preparation 10 minutes
Cooking 10 minutes
Serves 2

4 fresh sardines (or 2 x 100g can sardines)
olive oil, for drizzling
salt and freshly ground black pepper
4 slices good-quality bread, thickly sliced
lettuce of your choosing
½ red onion, finely sliced
2 large plum tomatoes, sliced

For the dressing

3–4 anchovy fillets, finely chopped
1 garlic clove, grated
2 teaspoons Dijon mustard
juice of 1 lemon
3 tablespoons olive oil

1 Preheat the grill to a high. Start by preparing the sardines. If you are using fresh, cut off the head and cut along the belly. Remove any guts and discard. Lay the fish on a board, belly-side down, and press firmly. This should open out the fish like a book – a preparation known as butterflying. Now turn the fish over, remove the backbone with your fingers and cut off the tail.

2 Once all the fillets are done, drizzle them with a little olive oil, season with salt and pepper and put them onto a very lightly oiled baking tray, ready for grilling.

3 To make the dressing, mix the chopped anchovies with the grated garlic, Dijon, lemon juice and the olive oil.

4 Grill the sardines for 5 minutes. There's no need to turn halfway as they are so thin.

5 Remove from the grill and lightly toast the bread on one side only. Drizzle one half of the bread with a little of the dressing, top with lettuce, sliced onion and tomato and, finally, the grilled sardines. Drizzle with the remaining dressing and put the remaining slice of toast on top. Eat while warm. If using canned sardines, pour away any water or oil from the can and remove any bones that may be in the fillets. Mash the sardines with a fork and pour over half the dressing. Spoon onto the untoasted side of the bread. Grill until warm. Build the sandwich as instructed above.

TIP I always have anchovies in my fridge as they add instant flavour to so many dishes, but if you don't have them or don't like them, feel free to leave them out of the dressing here.

Asian-style Salmon Fritters

I cook this dish as a starter quite often, as the majority of the cooking can be done in advance. You can use fresh or canned salmon, depending on your budget, and the fritters are also great as finger food for an informal occasion.

Preparation 20 minutes
Cooking 10 minutes
Serves 2–3

300g salmon, raw or canned
1 large egg yolk
1 tablespoon plain flour
2 tablespoons Thai Green Curry Paste, page 173, if you haven't made the curry paste use:
1 large chilli, a 2.5cm piece of ginger, peeled and grated, 2 garlic cloves, crushed, zest of 2 imes, 30g freshly chopped coriander leaves)
3 tablespoons vegetable oil

For the salad
¼ white cabbage, finely shredded
2 carrots, peeled and grated
3 plum tomatoes, deseeded and cut into thin strips
2 spring onions, finely sliced
1 eating apple (e.g. a sour Granny Smith), grated

For the dressing
zest and juice of 2 limes
2 tablespoons sweet chilli sauce
½ teaspoon chilli flakes
1 teaspoon sugar

To serve
lime wedges

1 Make the fritters first by placing the salmon, egg yolk, flour and Thai Green Curry Paste (or alternative ingredients) into a food processor and blend to a roughly textured paste. Divide the mixture into six equal portions, shape them into patties and put on a tray. You can put this in the fridge while you prepare the salad.

2 Make the dressing by combining all the ingredients in a bowl and set aside. To make the salad, combine the prepared vegetables and apple with the dressing in a large bowl. (This will now stay fresh for a few hours if well covered.)

3 When you are ready to serve, heat the oil in a frying pan and add the salmon fritters. Fry for 2–3 minutes per side before serving with the crispy, crunchy salad and a wedge of lime.

TIP These fritters are also great made with minced chicken or pork, just remember to give them an extra few minutes in the pan if your meat is raw!

Paprika and Orange Mackerel

I once had a dish very similar to this in a little family-run tapas bar in Spain that has stayed with me. Mackerel is a fish that isn't used nearly as much as I think it should be. When eaten fresh, it has the most wonderful flavour that is robust enough to hold its own among big flavours like these.

Preparation 5 minutes
Cooking 10 minutes
Serves 4

2 teaspoons smoked paprika
2 tablespoons plain flour
4 mackerel fillets
2 tablespoons olive oil
zest and juice of 1 orange
1 tablespoon clear honey
50g pine nuts, toasted (optional)
30g fresh coriander leaves, torn

1 Combine the paprika and the flour and dust the mackerel fillets in the mixture on both sides. Heat a frying pan with the oil and fry the fillets skin-side down for 3–4 minutes before turning and cooking the other side.

2 Add the orange zest and juice and honey to the pan and allow to bubble. Scatter over the toasted pine nuts, if using, and the torn coriander. Serve while hot.

TIP This dish makes a brilliant salad if you have any mackerel left over or got a deal on them so you bought a few more.

Maryland Sweet Potato Fishcakes

The worst part about making fishcakes is having to make the mash first. This recipe uses sweet potatoes because they cook very quickly and are cheap, but you can use leftover mash and swede to make these tasty cakes. Fishcakes are brilliant to make in bulk as they freeze really well and, if you buy fish that is not overly expensive, they can be made for next to nothing.

Preparation 45 minutes
Cooking 15 minutes
Serves 4

3–4 medium sweet potatoes
olive oil, for drizzling
salt and freshly ground black pepper
1 medium red chilli
125g sweetcorn (frozen or canned)
30g chopped coriander
500g white fish such as coley, pollock or
whiting, skinned and de-boned
2 large eggs
100g plain flour, plus extra for dusting
100g dried breadcrumbs, polenta or matzo meal
50ml vegetable oil, for frying

TIP These cakes are also
great as a veggie option
without the fish either as a
side dish or simply on their
own with a big squirt of
tomato ketchup.

1 Preheat the oven to 190°C/Gas 5. Cut the sweet potatoes in half and put them in a roasting tin. Drizzle with a little oil and season with salt and pepper. Put the tray in the preheated oven and cook for 25–30 minutes until the potatoes are cooked through and tender. Set aside and allow to cool. Leave the oven on to cook the fishcakes later.

2 Put the chilli, sweetcorn and coriander in a food processor and blend to a rough paste. (This can also be done by hand if you prefer.) Add the fish and blitz until just combined so that the fish still has some texture to it. Tip into a large bowl.

3 Scoop the sweet potato flesh from the skins using a spoon and combine with the fish mixture. If the mixture is still as little wet add some extra flour. Season well and mix. Divide the mixture into eight portions and shape them into patties. Chill in the fridge or freezer to firm up for about 15 minutes if you have time.

4 Beat the eggs in a bowl. Put the flour into another bowl and the breadcrumbs in another. Dip each patty in the flour, followed by the beaten egg, then the breadcrumbs. Ensure they are all well coated. These can now be frozen and cooked at a later date or cooked straightaway.

5 Heat the oil in a large non-stick frying pan. Add the fishcakes and cook until golden brown. Transfer to a baking tray and finish cooking them in the hot oven for a further 10 minutes. Serve the fishcakes with peas and broccoli.

Smoked Mackerel and Caper Pâté

This makes a perfect little starter for a dinner party on a budget. You can make it a couple of days ahead if you wish. If you have any left over, it works really well in sandwiches or spread onto toasted crostini for a simple but very tasty canapé or snack.

Preparation 10 minutes
Setting 20 minutes
Makes 6 small ramekins of pâté

4 smoked mackerel fillets, skin off
zest and juice of 1 lemon
100g cream cheese
1 tablespoon capers in vinegar
20g chopped dill
1 tablespoon horseradish sauce
salt and freshly ground black pepper

To serve

12 slices Melba toast or toasted rye
100g mini gherkins, cornichons,
or caper berries

1 Put all the ingredients in a food processor and whizz until combined but not totally puréed. It's nice to have a little texture in the pâté.

2 Spoon into ramekins and leave to chill in the fridge for a minimum of 20 minutes. Serve with Melba toast or toasted rye and a few pickled cornichons.

TIP Try serving these in little Kilner jars if you have them to make this very easy and cheap dish look even more impressive.

TIP Also great made with smoked salmon or trout instead of mackerel.

Tray-baked Ginger-glazed Salmon

You can cook this dish using a whole piece of salmon, supremes or fillets. It's so quick to make and requires very few ingredients. Salmon is widely available and probably the most frequently cooked fish in our kitchens, so I'm sure we're all in need of a little inspiration.

Preparation 5 minutes
Cooking 15–20 minutes
Serves 4–6

600–800g salmon fillet or supremes, skin on or off
2 tablespoons dark soy sauce
2 tablespoons stem ginger syrup
2 pieces stem ginger, cut into fine strips
juice and zest of 1 lime

1 Preheat the oven to 190°C/Gas 5. Line a baking tray with greaseproof paper and lay the salmon fillet or supremes on top.

2 Combine the remaining ingredients in a small bowl and pour or brush onto the salmon fillets on the flesh side only. Bake for 15–20 minutes if you have a whole, large piece of fish, or 8–10 minutes for smaller pieces. You will know that the fish is cooked when you can easily flake the flesh using a fork.

3 Remove from the oven and flake the fish, if you wish, before serving with either steamed rice, stir-fried vegetables or Singapore Noodles (see page 110).

TIPS Make a little extra of the marinade and add some sliced garlic and a pinch of chilli flakes. Blanch some broccoli before stir-frying with the marinade for a delicious accompaniment.

Pulses, Grains and Pasta

Pulses, Grains and Pasta

This chapter is all about how to make the most of what is in your kitchen cupboards. Whether it's couscous, lentils or chickpeas most of us usually have some kind of pasta, pulses or grains to hand.

I'm a huge fan of pulses, grains and pasta. They keep for months, even years, in the cupboard without going off or deteriorating in quality. They are cheap to buy, especially if you shop cleverly and restock when there are deals on cans in your local supermarket. You get a lot for your money and a little really does go a long way – essential for when you are trying to cook on a budget.

I simply love pasta and it's always in my cupboard. I prefer the texture of dried pasta to the fresh kind available from the chilled section in shops and it's also a lot more economical, plus it lasts, so there's no danger of any waste. A comforting bowl of pasta is the perfect weeknight meal and can be thrown together using whatever fresh ingredients you have to hand, such as the Cherry Tomato, Ricotta and Basil Linguine (see page 92).

When it comes to pulses I tend to be less particular. I usually buy canned as they are a brilliant back-up option when you're running low on ingredients for a dish and need to bulk it out a little. As they are already cooked they also don't add any additional cooking time to the recipe. Simply take off the lid, rinse in cold water and make a delicious side of Moroccan Carrot and Chickpeas (see page 105), a hearty Black Bean Chilli (see page 118) or blitz with a few herbs and spices, pan-fry and serve with flatbread for a super quick and low cost Falafel (see page 113).

I do use dried pulses, but usually on a weekend when I have the time to soak and boil them. If you are feeling particularly thrifty, you can soak and boil the pulses in bulk and store them for up to four days in the fridge in an airtight container. When cooking with dried pulses do be aware that the older they are, the longer they will take to cook.

In these recipes most of the main ingredients are interchangeable – if I have suggested bulgar wheat but you only have pearl barley, or even just rice, in your cupboards then do use this instead. One of the keys to thrifty cooking is using what you have rather than going out and buying more ingredients and this is especially true when cooking with pasta, grains and pulses.

Pork Milanese with Marinara Spaghetti

This is such a great weeknight meal. I know the classic ingredient to use for this dish is veal, but veal is generally quite expensive and, although I'm not against eating it, it has to have been reared ethically and come under the bracket of 'rose'. Pork fillets are a great replacment if cooking on a shoestring and are the perfect substitute for veal.

Preparation 20 minutes
Cooking 30–40 minutes
Serves 4

For the Milanese

1 pork fillet (450g), cut into 8 medallions
6 tablespoons plain flour
salt and freshly ground black pepper
2 eggs, beaten
100g dried or fresh breadcrumbs
4 tablespoons vegetable oil

For the marinara sauce

1 tablespoon olive or vegetable oil
1 large onion, chopped
1 celery stick, chopped
3 garlic cloves, chopped
½ teaspoon dried chilli flakes
pinch of salt
1 tablespoon tomato purée
2 x 400g cans chopped or plum tomatoes
30g fresh basil leaves
a pinch of sugar, if needed

500g dried spaghetti

To serve (optional)
lemon wedges
grated Parmesan cheese

1 To make the sauce, put a pan on the hob and set to a medium heat. Add the oil, onion, celery, garlic, chilli flakes and salt and cook for 5–6 minutes before adding the tomato purée and tomatoes. Add half the basil and simmer for a minimum of 20 minutes. Add a pinch of sugar, if the sauce is a bit tart.

2 When you are happy that the sauce is ready, blend it, either with a hand-held blender or in a large blender (this part is optional – it's fine to have a chunky sauce). Put the sauce back into the pan and allow to simmer over a low heat.

3 Cook the pasta according to the packet instructions until al dente.

4 Now prepare the Milanese. Using a meat bat or rolling pin, beat each medallion of pork until it is thin and of an even thickness all over. You want them as thin as you can get them – about 1.5–2mm is good. Now dust each escalope in flour and season with salt and pepper, then dip them into the beaten eggs, then into the breadcrumbs. Ensure they are all well coated. (The coated escalopes can be frozen at this stage if you have made too many, providing the pork hasn't been previously frozen.)

5 Put a large frying pan on the hob and add half the oil. Lay in four of the eight escalopes and cook until golden. This will take about 4 minutes per side. Remove from the pan. Cook the other four with the remaining oil.

6 Once the pasta is cooked, drain it well and stir through the marinara sauce. Add the remaining basil leaves. To serve, pile the milanese on top of the spaghetti and garnish with a wedge of lemon and some grated Parmesan cheese.

Cherry Tomato, Ricotta and Basil Linguine

This is a seriously simple recipe, but that is what this book is about – simple things done well and on a budget. Ricotta might not be an ingredient that you use all the time but it is extremely versatile and will go with a whole variety of other recipes in this book – pretty much any salad (especially the Sweet Potato and Bulgar Wheat Salad, page 108), pasta dish or risotto will love this ingredient, not to mention eating it simply sweetened with a little icing sugar and served with some stewed fruits.

Preparation 5 minutes
Cooking 15 minutes
Serves 4

salt and freshly ground black pepper
500g linguine
75ml extra virgin olive oil
3 garlic cloves, chopped
½ teaspoon chilli flakes
700g cherry tomatoes, halved
200g ricotta cheese
15–20 fresh basil leaves

1 Put a large pan of water on the hob, add a pinch of salt and bring to the boil. Once boiling, add the linguine and cook according to the packet instructions until al dente.

2 Pour the oil into a large frying pan and add the garlic and chilli flakes. Cook for 2 minutes before adding the tomatoes, a large pinch of salt and a good couple of twists of black pepper. Allow the tomatoes to cook for 3–4 minutes. You don't want them to become mushy – they should still be quite firm, with a few starting to burst and ooze their lovely juices.

3 Once the pasta is cooked, drain it and add the tomatoes. Stir well before crumbling in the ricotta cheese and the basil leaves. Serve immediately.

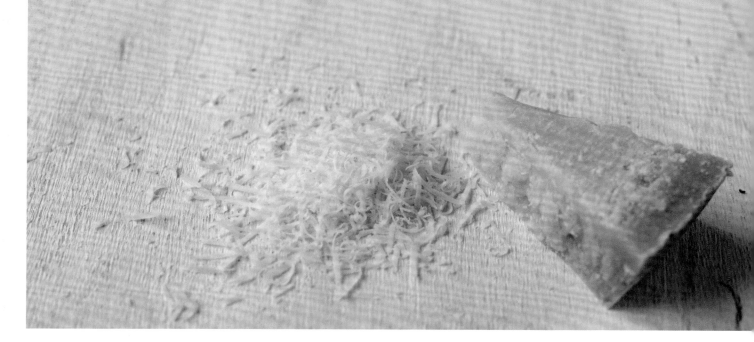

TIP Try to make this dish when cherry tomatoes are in season as they are 50 per cent cheaper. If you fancy this out of season, canned cherry tomatoes will do the job.

Courgette, Pesto and Ravioli Bake

My eyes often tend to be bigger than my belly and, when it comes to cooking pasta, I always cook too much. I can't help it. Even when I've weighed it beforehand, I can never allow myself to believe that it will be enough. Of course, I'm always wrong and end up with half a colander of leftover cooked pasta. Shop-bought ravioli or tortellini are no exception and I can never buy just one packet, so this is what I do the following day to use up the pasta that I cooked out of pure greed and couldn't finish.

Preparation 10 minutes
Cooking 30 minutes
Serves 4

500g fresh ravioli or tortellini
25g butter
25g plain flour
500ml milk
1 tablespoon Dijon mustard
salt and freshly ground black pepper
4 tablespoons pesto, homemade
(see page 173) or shop-bought
3 courgettes, grated
40g Parmesan cheese (or any cheese of your
choosing), grated

1 Preheat the oven to 180°C/Gas 4. Start by cooking the pasta if you're not using leftover cooked pasta. Cook to al dente, according to the packet instructions and leave to drain in a colander.

2 Next, make the sauce for the topping. Melt the butter in a small saucepan, then add the flour and mix to a paste. Cook for a few minutes before adding a third of the milk. Stir well until the mixture starts to boil, then add another third. Repeat the process before adding the final third along with the Dijon mustard. Season with salt and pepper.

3 Mix the pesto and the grated courgette through the cooked pasta and season with a little salt and pepper before transferring to a 30 x 20cm baking dish and pouring the white sauce over the top.

4 Sprinkle with grated Parmesan and bake for 20–25 minutes until golden brown.

TIP This recipe works well with stuffed pasta, but I often make it with the nearly-but-not-quite-finished packets of pasta of different shapes and sizes that I have hanging around in my cupboard. Have a go and make a mismatched pasta bake.

Gnocchi with Pesto and Chard

If you can boil a potato, you can make gnocchi. This kind of gnocchi can be boiled, pan-fried or baked and is a great substitute for pasta on a weeknight. Feel free to be adventurous and add whatever herbs or spices suit your taste and, of course, the sauce is your choice.

Preparation 40 minutes
Cooking 10 minutes
Serves 4 as a main course, 6 as a starter

750g floury potatoes, unpeeled
2 large egg yolks
150g plain flour, plus extra for dusting
75g grated Parmesan cheese,
plus extra to serve (optional)
salt and freshly ground black pepper
300g Swiss chard with stalks,
or spring greens
1 tablespoon olive oil, plus extra for drizzling
1 portion of Pesto from page 173, or
3 tablespoons shop-bought
zest of 1 lemon

1 Put the unpeeled whole potatoes in a pan of salted water, bring to the boil and cook until tender – about 25 minutes. Once cooked, remove the potatoes from the pan and leave until cool enough to handle. I'm impatient so I often hold them in a clean tea towel to peel them. Use a little knife to pull the skin away from the flesh.

2 Pass the potatoes through a ricer into a large bowl or mash well – no lumps, please! Now make a well in the centre of the mashed potatoes and add the egg yolks, half the flour and the Parmesan. Season with salt and pepper and start to mix the contents of the bowl from the inside out – you need to use your hands to make this dish. Add more flour as you go. You may not need it all or you may need a little more – it very much depends on which potatoes you have. The mixture should be coming away from the sides of the bowl and sticking together nicely when moulded.

3 Remove the potato dough from the bowl and put onto a floured surface. Divide the mix into four and roll each into a long sausage. Cut the gnocchi to your desired size. I prefer mine a little smaller than usual – about 1.5cm each. Leave the gnocchi to rest in the fridge while you make the chard.

4 Chop the chard into bite-sized pieces about the same size as the gnocchi. Heat a frying pan with a little olive oil and cook the stalks for 3 minutes, followed by the leaves. Once the leaves are wilted, turn off the heat while you cook the gnocchi.

5 Bring a pan of water to the boil and season with salt. Add the gnocchi and cook until they float to the surface, then remove from the water and drain well. Coat the gnocchi in the pesto and stir through the chard.

6 Add the lemon zest and serve. Add more grated Parmesan and a drizzle of olive oil, if you wish.

Sausage Meatball Carbonara

We all need a few different pasta dishes in our repertoire that we can throw together quickly and cheaply, with little fuss. It's got to be a hit with all the family, which this one is definitely going to be: sausages - good; pasta - good; cream - good. It's also really important to not have to buy huge amounts of different ingredients for a weeknight supper, so I hope with this recipe you don't have to deviate from your basic shop too much.

Preparation 15 minutes
Cooking 15 minutes
Serves 4

4 good-quality meaty pork sausages
salt and freshly ground black pepper
500g pasta (such as rigatoni or penne)
1 tablespoon olive oil
2 garlic cloves, chopped
½ teaspoon chilli flakes
4 tablespoons crème fraîche
zest of 2 lemons
30g freshly chopped parsley leaves
50g Parmesan, grated

1 Remove the sausagemeat from the skins and put into a bowl. Wet your hands to prevent the meat sticking to you too much and roll the sausagemeat into 20 or so little mini meatballs.

2 Put a large pan of salted water on the hob and bring to the boil, then cook the pasta according to the packet instructions until al dente.

3 Put a frying pan over a medium heat and add the oil. Gently fry the meatballs for about 5–6 minutes until they start to go golden brown. Add the garlic and chilli flakes and cook for 3–4 minutes, then turn the heat to low and add the crème fraîche. Simmer for a further 5–6 minutes. Ensure the sauce doesn't boil at this stage.

4 Once the pasta is cooked, drain well and stir it through the meatball sauce, add the lemon zest, chopped parsley and Parmesan. Season with black pepper just before you serve.

Greek-style Rice Salad

I often make this quick and healthy salad when I'm home alone. It's made using things that most of us will have in our fridges. You may not usually have feta cheese, but I do advise that you make it one of your weekly staples. Feta cheese will instantly liven up any cold salad and it has a pretty long shelf life, so you don't have to worry about it going off before you use it. The great thing about using a strong, salty cheese such as feta is that a little goes a long way, so you don't need very much to make an impact. If you don't want to use feta you could use goat's cheese, Boursin or even some grilled halloumi.

Preparation 15 minutes
Cooking 15 minutes
Serves 4 as a light lunch,
or 6 as a side salad

200g rice (I like to use red rice, but whatever you have is fine)
1 medium cucumber, deseeded and cut into 1cm pieces
2 large tomatoes, quartered, deseeded and cut into thin strips
75g black pitted olives, sliced
½ red onion, finely sliced
200g feta cheese
salt and freshly ground black pepper
30g fresh basil or parsley leaves, roughly chopped (optional)

For the dressing
3 teaspoons red wine vinegar
1 heaped teaspoon Dijon mustard
4 tablespoons olive oil

To serve (optional)
1 lemon, quartered

1 Boil the rice as instructed on the packet until tender, drain and leave to cool.

2 Mix the chopped vegetables with the cooled rice. Crumble in the feta, trying to keep the pieces quite big. Season with pepper and a little salt, but go easy, as the feta is already quite salty.

3 Make the dressing by combining all the ingredients together in a jug or bowl. Pour the dressing over the rice salad. Add the herbs once ready to serve, mix well and pile onto plates or a flat serving platter. Serve with lemon wedges if you wish.

TIP I often have this with some griddled pitta and some hummus if I want to bulk it out a bit.

Broccoli and Blue Cheese Risotto

Risottos are perfect for using up bits and pieces you may have in your fridge that have been slightly neglected. There's always some broccoli in my fridge, but as there are only two of us, I'm often left with half a head by the end of the week. I have chosen to team up my broccoli risotto with blue cheese — a classic combination — but you can, of course, use whatever cheese ends you happen to have left after a cheese-board frenzy.

Preparation 15 minutes
Cooking 25–30 minutes
Serves 2

400g broccoli florets, cooked
750ml hot vegetable or chicken stock
(homemade or shop-bought is fine)
2 tablespoons olive oil
1 onion, finely chopped
2 garlic cloves, chopped
salt and freshly ground black pepper
150g arborio rice
150ml white wine
75g blue cheese, or any strong cheese
of your choice
25g butter

To serve
grated or shaved Parmesan (optional)

1 Blend two-thirds of the cooked broccoli florets with 250ml of the stock to make a paste. You don't need it to be completely smooth. This can be done in a blender or food processor.

2 Put a large sauté pan or deep frying pan on the hob, add the olive oil and turn the heat to medium. Add the onion, garlic and a large pinch of salt and cook for 3–4 minutes. When the onion is soft, add the rice and stir for a few minutes before adding the white wine. Stir the risotto continuously until all the wine has been absorbed by the rice. Now add the hot stock, one ladleful at a time, and keep stirring. Once each ladleful has been absorbed, add another.

3 The rice should take about 17–20 minutes to cook. Once you are happy with the texture and consistency (it should be thick and creamy and the rice slightly al dente), add the broccoli purée along with the larger broccoli florets and crumble in the cheese (use the rind as well, as long as it isn't too dry). Stir well and season before adding the butter.

4 Serve straightaway with some shaved or grated Parmesan if you wish.

TIP You can add pretty much any ingredient to a risotto; if you have a leek, celery, carrot or even courgette, finely chop it and add it along with the onion in step 2.

Mussel and Tomato Baked Risotto

Mussels are one of the cheapest ingredients from the sea that you can get hold of. You get loads for your money and can do so much with them. Baked, stir-fried, braised or boiled, they can be used to make a welcome dish on just about any seafood lover's table minus the usual hefty price tag.

Preparation 15 minutes
Cooking 45–50 minutes
Serves 6

2 tablespoons olive oil
1 onion, chopped
3 garlic cloves, finely chopped or sliced
1 teaspoon chilli flakes
1 heaped teaspoon smoked paprika, or any paprika you have
1 teaspoon dried mixed herbs or oregano
salt and freshly ground black pepper
300g risotto rice or paella rice
100ml white wine
1kg cleaned, live mussels
1 tablespoon tomato purée
2 x 400g cans chopped tomatoes (canned cherry tomatoes also work very well here if you have them)
600ml fish, chicken or vegetable stock

To serve
freshly chopped flatleaf parsley
lemon wedges (optional)

1 Preheat the oven to 180°C/Gas 4. Put a flameproof casserole or sauté dish (preferably one with a lid) on the hob and add the oil. Set the heat to medium and add the onion, garlic and chilli flakes. Cook for 3–5 minutes before adding the paprika and dried herbs. Season with salt and pepper before adding the rice. Coat the rice well in all the spices, then add the wine.

2 Cook for 3–5 minutes to allow the wine to reduce by half before adding the mussels (if you are using frozen seafood (see tip, below), don't add this yet), tomato purée, canned tomatoes and all of the stock. Bring to the boil, put a lid on top and transfer to the oven for 35 minutes. (If you don't have a lid, cover tightly with kitchen foil.) Check on the risotto halfway through cooking as you may need to add a splash more stock. If you are using frozen seafood make sure it is thoroughly defrosted and add it now.

3 The dish is ready when the rice is soft and all the mussels have opened. Remove from the oven and serve with a sprinkling of parsley and a wedge of lemon, if you so wish.

TIP If you can't get hold of live mussels, try this recipe with a defrosted frozen seafood mix. It's also very tasty.

Arancini

This is the only way to use up leftover risotto of any flavour. Simply shape the risotto into balls, fill with a little cheese, coat in breadcrumbs and fry them. Serve with a spicy hot tomato sauce as a little start to your dinner party or a Saturday afternoon treat.

Preparation 15 minutes
Cooking 10 minutes
Makes 12 bite-sized balls

400g leftover risotto
75g soft cheese such as Boursin or
Philadelphia, Gorgonzola, soft goat's cheese
or mozzarella
5 tablespoons plain flour
2 eggs, beaten
100g dried breadcrumbs
300ml vegetable oil, for frying
sea salt

TIP These can be made using any leftover risotto from page 101 or 102.

1 The leftover risotto should be completely cold and set hard; divide it into 12 equally sized balls or as many as you can from the leftovers. Make a dent in the centre of each one and add 1 teaspoon of your chosen cheese. Tightly close the rice around the filling so that it doesn't all leak out as it heats up. It may help if you have wet hands to do this to stop the rice from sticking to them too much.

2 Put the flour into a bowl, the beaten eggs into another and the breadcrumbs into a third. Roll the little arancini balls first in the flour, then dip into the egg and finally roll in the breadcrumbs. Ensure they are well coated. These can be put into the fridge for up to two days and cooked later or can be cooked straightaway.

3 Heat the oil to 190°C. You can test the temperature by carefully dropping a small piece of bread into the oil – if it bubbles and goes golden brown instantly, the oil is hot enough. Put the arancini onto a slotted spoon and very gently lower them into the hot oil. Cook for about 5–6 minutes until they are golden brown all over. Remove them from the oil using the slotted spoon again and drain on kitchen paper.

4 Season with a little sea salt and serve with a portion of the Bravas Sauce (see page 134).

Moroccan Carrot and Chickpeas

While this cheap, quick and super-healthy dish is great the day it's made, it's even better once it's had a few days of marinating, so it's a good dish to make in bulk. I suggest that the sauce from my Lamb Shoulder Shank Tagine on page 26 would make a great addition to this salad, so why not have a go and marry the pair up?

Preparation 15 minutes
Serves 4

1 x 400g can chickpeas, cooked and drained
(or 200g dried chickpeas soaked overnight in
cold water and cooked in clean water for
1 hour or until tender)
4 large carrots, peeled and grated
1 garlic clove, grated
2.5cm piece of fresh ginger, peeled and grated
75g dried sultanas, raisins or
chopped apricots
juice and zest of 1 lemon
1 teaspoon ground cumin
4 tablespoons olive oil
30g fresh coriander, mint or parsley leaves,
finely shredded
salt and freshly ground black pepper

1 Put the chickpeas in a large bowl. Add the grated carrot, garlic, ginger, dried fruit, lemon juice and zest, cumin, olive oil and herbs. Season with salt and pepper and mix well. Serve.

Pineapple Fried Rice

Have a go at pairing this delicious rice dish with a grilled gammon steak — it tastes amazing. The sweetness of the pineapple works perfectly with the salty gammon. The sharpness of the pineapple is a welcome treat and helps to cut through the richness of a gammon steak but it is just as tasty served on its own to make the most of ingredients from your cupboards and freezer.

Preparation 20 minutes
Cooking 30 minutes
Serves 4

350g white rice
2 tablespoons vegetable oil
3 eggs
2 garlic cloves, finely chopped
2.5cm piece of fresh ginger, peeled and finely chopped or grated
1 red or green chilli, chopped or 1½ teaspoons chilli flakes
8 spring onions, chopped
200g pineapple, either canned chunks cut into bite-sized pieces or you can use fresh, peeled and cut the same way
100g frozen peas
4 tablespoons light soy sauce
2 tablespoons sweet chilli sauce
juice of 1 lime

To serve
4 lime wedges
coriander leaves, torn (optional)

1 Start by cooking the rice according to the packet instructions. Drain in a colander and set aside to cool completely.

2 Heat a large frying pan or wok and add 1 tablespoon of the oil. When hot, crack the eggs into the wok and scramble for about 3–4 minutes until the eggs are set. Remove them from the pan and set aside.

3 Now add the remaining tablespoon of oil to the wok and add the garlic, ginger and chilli and stir-fry for a few minutes before adding the chopped spring onions, pineapple, the frozen peas and cooked egg. Mix together well.

4 Add the soy sauce and sweet chilli. Coat everything in the wok in the sauce before adding the cooked rice and the lime juice.

5 Serve the rice with a wedge of lime and the coriander, if you like.

TIP If you have a stash of ready-puréed garlic, ginger and chilli in the fridge or freezer, use these in place of the fresh flavourings.

Sweet Potato and Bulgar Wheat Salad with Pomegranate

This recipe is not only great as a lunch or dinner, but also as an accompaniment to barbecued dishes on a summer's day. It's perfect on its own or with a few slices of grilled halloumi. All the ingredients are easy to pick up and are cheap, especially when in season.

Preparation 10 minutes
Cooking 25 minutes
Serves 2

1 red onion, peeled and cut into 6–8 wedges
2 sweet potatoes (skin on),
each cut into 6–8 wedges
salt and freshly ground black pepper
2 teaspoons ground cumin
2 tablespoons olive oil
100g bulgar wheat
chicken or vegetable stock cube (optional)
zest and juice of 1 orange
2 tablespoons freshly chopped herbs such as
parsley, coriander, basil or mint leaves
(frozen is fine)
110g pomegranate seeds

1 Preheat the oven to 180°C/Gas 4. Put the red onion and sweet potato wedges on a non-stick baking tray. Season with salt and pepper, sprinkle over the cumin and drizzle with the olive oil. Bake for 25 minutes, turning once during cooking.

2 Pour the bulgar wheat into a saucepan and cover with water. Add a pinch of salt or a chicken or vegetable stock cube, if you have one. Bring to the boil and cook for 8 minutes. Once cooked, drain and set aside.

3 When the onions and sweet potatoes are cooked, fold them through the cooked bulgar wheat. Add the orange zest and juice, the chopped herbs and the pomegranate seeds and stir well. Serve just as it is, or with some slices of grilled halloumi cheese.

Singapore Noodles

This is the only dish I need if I'm having a Chinese takeaway and my own version is just as good.

Preparation 15 minutes
Cooking 20 minutes
Serves 4 as a main course, or
6 as a side dish

350g vermicelli rice noodles or glass noodles
2 tablespoons vegetable oil
8 spring onions, sliced, white and
green parts separated
2 red peppers, sliced
250g Atlantic prawns
150–200g cooked chicken, pork or beef,
shredded (optional)
4 eggs, beaten
4 tablespoons soy sauce

Paste for noodles
4cm piece of fresh ginger, peeled
4 garlic cloves, peeled
2 medium-hot green or red chillies
3 teaspoons medium-hot curry powder
3 teaspoons turmeric

To serve (optional)
fresh coriander leaves
4 lime wedges

1 Start by making the paste. Blend all the paste ingredients together using a mortar and pestle or a mini-blender. You want the paste to be as smooth as possible. If you find it's not quite getting there, add a little vegetable oil or water to help it on its way. Set aside.

2 Cook the vermicelli or glass noodles according to the packet instructions. (If you have bought fresh noodles from the chilled section, you don't need to do this.)

3 Heat up a wok or large frying pan and add half the vegetable oil. Once hot, add the white parts of the spring onions (reserve the green tips for later) and the sliced peppers. Cook these for 3–5 minutes before adding the paste, then cook for a further 5–6 minutes. Add the prawns and any cooked meat you have and mix well. Scoop this from the pan or wok into a bowl and set aside.

4 Add the remaining oil to the pan, ensure it is really hot, then add all the beaten egg. Leave the egg to set in the pan for 20–30 seconds or so before you start to scramble them using a wooden spoon. Once the egg is thoroughly cooked (this will take about 2 minutes), add the spring onion and prawn mix back into the wok along with the noodles. Add the soy sauce and the remaining green parts of the spring onions. Stir well.

5 Serve garnished with freshly torn coriander and a wedge of lime, if you wish. These noodles go really well with the Tray-baked Ginger-glazed Salmon on page 86.

TIP This dish is a great way of using up any leftovers — shredded chicken, beef, pork, lamb or simply cooked vegetables. Just throw it all in and try to make sure it's all cut to about the same size.

Chickpea Cakes (Falafel)

Falafel are a staple in our household. I find it reassuring to know that as long as I have a can of chickpeas, I can always create a great cheap, healthy and tasty meal in a flash. These patties are perfect as a dinner-party starter on a shoestring, finger food with friends or to snack on in front of the telly while the football is on.

Preparation 10 minutes
Cooking 5 minutes
Makes 8 small cakes

For the falafel

1 x 400g can chickpeas, rinsed and drained (or
200g dried soaked overnight in cold water and
cooked in clean water for 1 hour
or until tender)
2 garlic cloves, crushed
½ teaspoon chilli powder
1 teaspoon ground cumin
1 teaspoon ground coriander
1 tablespoon freshly chopped parsley,
coriander or mint leaves
2 tablespoons plain flour
salt and freshly ground black pepper
3 tablespoons vegetable oil

For the coating

3 tablespoons plain flour
1 egg, beaten
3 tablespoons dried breadcrumbs or polenta

To serve (optional)

hummus or Greek yogurt
mini pitta breads or flatbreads
4 lemon wedges

1 Put all the ingredients for the falafel except the oil in a food processor. Season with salt and pepper. Blend to a smooth paste, then divide the mixture into eight portions. Mould each portion into a patty shape. Put the flour into a small bowl, the beaten egg into another and the breadcrumbs into a third. Roll the patties in the flour, then dip in the egg and, finally, roll in the breadcrumbs.

2 Heat a large frying pan. Add the oil and the coated patties and fry for 2–3 minutes on each side until they are golden brown. Serve with a hummus or yogurt dip and some toasted pitta or flatbreads, if you wish, but they are also delicious just as they are with a little wedge of lemon.

TIP This recipe is also great
with kidney beans instead of chickpeas
if you've forgotten to restock.

Spicy Beans and Pepperoni on Toast with Fried Egg

On toast, in jackets or served as a soup, this savvy saver's dish is quick, cheap and cheerful. You can make it with dried or canned beans, fresh tomatoes, jarred artisan pepperoni that needs using up or your everyday lunchbox type. It's your recipe; I'm just giving you the method. You can choose what exactly to put in it using my guidelines and with an eye on what needs using up in your kitchen.

Preparation 10 minutes
Cooking 15 minutes
Serves 2

75g Peperami, cut into 0.5cm pieces (you can also use pepperoni, chorizo or even pancetta)
2 garlic cloves, chopped
1 fresh red chilli, chopped
1 x 400g can haricot beans
200ml passata or 1 x 400g can chopped tomatoes (if you don't have either use a 2 tablespoons tomato purée and add 200ml water)
salt and freshly ground black pepper
a pinch of sugar if needed
1 tablespoon vegetable or sunflower oil, for frying
2 fresh eggs
2–4 slices bread of your choice
butter, to spread on toast

To serve (optional)
pinch of ground cumin
fresh coriander leaves, roughly chopped

1 Put a non-stick medium saucepan on the hob and set the heat to low. Add the Peperami and cook for a few minutes. Once the fat starts melting from the sausage, add the garlic and chilli, followed by the beans. Stir the mixture well before adding the passata or chopped tomatoes. If you have any fresh cherry tomatoes or larger chopped tomatoes that need using up, throw them in now. Season with salt and pepper. Have a taste to check if the stew is a bit tart and, if it is, add a pinch of sugar and cook for 10 minutes on a low simmer while you fry the eggs and toast the bread.

2 To fry the eggs, heat the oil in a non-stick frying pan. Crack in the eggs and cook over a medium heat for 4–5 minutes until the white is set but the yolk is still runny.

3 Toast the bread, butter it and divide it between two plates.

4 Divide the beans equally over the slices of toast. Top each portion of beans with an egg, sunny-side up.

5 If you have it, add a small pinch of cumin and salt to the top of each yolk, then sprinkle over some fresh coriander if you like, and serve immediately.

TIP If you don't fancy these beans
on toast but like the sound of the
ingredients why not make it into a hearty
soup. Simply add a little more passata or
canned tomatoes and a splash (100ml) of
vegetable or chicken stock. Serve with a
spoonful of soured cream and some grated
cheese if you wish.

Barley and Curried Squash Soup

This combination makes a great salad as well as a delicious soup that's substantial enough for an evening meal as it's very filling, although I always seem to manage a chunk of crusty bread on the side. Make the soup in batches and freeze them — it is so great to come home and know you have a home-cooked, healthy meal ready without any fuss and with no expense.

Preparation 10 minutes
Cooking 35 minutes
Serves 6–8

1 tablespoon vegetable oil
1 large onion, roughly chopped
1 celery stick, roughly chopped
salt and freshly ground black pepper
2.cm piece of fresh ginger, grated
2 garlic cloves, chopped
2 teaspoons mild curry powder
1 large butternut squash, chopped into small dice (seeds removed)
1 litre vegetable stock
125g pearl barley
a squeeze of lemon juice

To serve (optional)
crumbled feta or goat's cheese
pumpkin seeds

1 Put a large flameproof casserole on the hob and add the oil. Add the chopped onion and celery and cook for 6–8 minutes, covered.

2 Season with salt and pepper before adding the grated ginger and garlic along with the curry powder. Cook the spices for a few minutes before adding the butternut squash and the stock. Put the lid back on and simmer for 25 minutes.

3 While the soup is cooking, boil the pearl barley in a separate saucepan of boiling water until tender. This should take about 15 minutes.

4 Once the vegetables are tender purée the soup using a hand-held blender, or by transferring the contents of the pan to a food processor. Ensure you don't get splashed by any of the hot soup. Blitz the soup until it is completely smooth.

5 Drain the pearl barley and add it to the puréed soup. Add a squeeze of lemon juice and check again for seasoning.

6 If you have any feta or goat's cheese, crumble a little over each serving and sprinkle over a few pumpkin seeds for extra texture and little bit of creaminess.

TIP To try this as a salad, rub the squash with the spices and roast for 20–25 minutes at 180C/Gas 4. Mix with the cooked barley and finish with some crumbled goat's cheese.

TIP Substitute the
pearl barley with
red lentils or a
can of chickpeas,
if you fancy.

Black Bean Chilli

We all know how to make chilli con carne — well, this is a version of that very popular in Mexican street food and is used in a whole host of different traditional recipes. This recipe is lovely just with rice, but it can also be adapted to make burritos or enchiladas.

Preparation 10 minutes
Cooking 40–50 minutes
Serves 6

2 teaspoons olive oil
2 garlic cloves, chopped
1 large red onion, chopped
2 large red chillies, chopped
salt and freshly ground black pepper
3 teaspoons ground cumin
¼ teaspoon cinnamon or 1 cinnnamon stick
2 teaspoons medium paprika
½ teaspoon hot chilli powder
1 tablespoon tomato purée
2 x 400g cans black beans, drained
(or use aduki beans)
1x 400g can red kidney beans, drained
2 x 400g cans chopped tomatoes
250ml vegetable or chicken stock

To serve
boiled rice
2 spring onions, chopped
6 lime wedges
grated or crumbled feta or goat's cheese
(optional)

1 Put a large saucepan on the hob over a low heat and add the olive oil. Once the oil is hot, add the garlic, onion, chilli and a pinch of salt and cook for 5–6 minutes.

2 Now add the cumin, cinnamon, paprika and chilli powder along with the tomato purée. Stir well and cook the spices for a few minutes before adding the canned beans, canned tomatoes and stock. Slowly bring the stew to the boil and cook for 30–40 minutes. Season to taste.

3 Serve with boiled rice, some chopped spring onions, lime wedges and some grated or crumbled feta, if you have it.

TIP Try adding some shredded pork belly to this recipe from page 34 or if you don't have that some cooked chicken or even some spicy sausage will work equally as well for an interesting and tasty twist. Or simply spoon these perfectly spiced beans over some tortilla crisps, sprinkle with cheese and grill. Soured cream is essential!

TIP Try making some guacamole if you have an unhappy avocado lying about.

Storecupboard Granola

We all have those half packs of dried fruits, nuts and seeds from recipes that we cooked only once. Use them up in this recipe instead of waiting for the bag to annoyingly split, and spending 20 minutes sweeping sesame seeds out of your drawer. It's a healthy and delicious start to the day served with yogurt, on porridge or tossed with some marinated berries (see page 138).

Preparation 5 minutes
Cooking 30 minutes
Makes about 700g

2 tablespoons vegetable oil
6 tablespoons of clear honey or maple syrup
300g rolled oats (porridge oats are fine)
300g nuts and seeds, such as almonds,
pecan nuts, pistachio nuts, sunflower seeds,
pumpkin seeds and sesame seed)
125g dried fruits, such as cranberries,
sultanas, chopped apricots

1 Preheat the oven to 180°C/Gas 4. Line a baking tray with greaseproof paper.

2 Mix the oil, honey or maple syrup, oats, nuts and seeds in a bowl and mix well. Spread the mixture onto the lined baking tray and bake for 15 minutes.

3 Remove the tray from the oven and add the fruit. Mix it all well and bake for another 10 minutes.

4 Remove from the oven and leave to cool before storing away for your next breakfast treat. It will keep for up to one month in an airtight container.

TIP Stir this through some vanilla ice cream for a cheeky midnight feast.

Salted Caramel Popcorn

A trip to the cinema in our house does tend to start off on the wrong foot. Not because his choice of movie tends to always include at least 20 minutes worth of car chase, 20 minutes of on-screen nudity and another 20 minutes of some muscular hero saving the world (well, the muscular hero bit I can cope with), or because I like diet coke and he prefers normal Coca-Cola. I am totally prepared to compromise on all these minor differences, but salted popcorn? Really, that's one compromise I just can't make. Therefore, I decided to come up with my own solution.

Cooking 15 minutes
Makes 2 large bowls

3 tablespoons vegetable or sunflower oil
½ teaspoon salt
75g popcorn kernels

For the salted caramel coating
100g salted butter
150g light brown sugar
3 tablespoons golden syrup
1½ teaspoons sea salt flakes (not table salt)
½ teaspoon baking powder or
bicarbonate of soda

1 Preheat the oven to 140°C/Gas 1. First you need to pop the corn. Put your largest pan on the hob – it is essential you have a tight-fitting lid for this recipe. Add the oil and salt along with 2 tablespoons of the popcorn kernels and put on the lid. Set the heat to high and wait for the popping sound. As soon as you hear it, remove the pan from the heat, add the remaining popcorn kernels and wait for 30 seconds. (I do this so that all the kernels pop and the popcorn doesn't burn at the bottom. This way all the kernels should pop at the same time once back on the heat.)

2 After 30 seconds, put the pan back over a high heat, leave the lid very slightly off to allow steam to escape and allow the popping to start. Gently shake the pan while it cooks. Once cooked, transfer the popcorn to two large bowls and leave to cool while you make the sauce.

3 Heat the butter, sugar and golden syrup in a pan until melted, then reduce the heat and simmer for 3–4 minutes. Stir in the salt and the baking powder; the mixture will bubble as you do this, so do it carefully. Then pour the sauce all over the popcorn and mix well with a wooden spoon. Transfer the coated popcorn onto two baking trays and cook in the oven for 15 minutes to dry it out.

4 Allow the popcorn to cool slightly before eating.

Fruit and Vegetables

Fruit and Vegetables

We are spoilt for choice with the selection of fruit and vegetables that are available to us. There is almost nothing that we can't buy pretty much all year round and because of this our natural instinct to buy more can sometimes be overwhelming. All too often we buy ingredients we don't actually need or have any plans to use just because they are on offer or look so appetising. You buy two punnets of raspberries and the first one goes perfectly with your yogurt and granola for breakfast on Sunday but the second gets forgotten about at the back of the fridge, eventually starts sprouting green fluff and ultimately gets thrown out with the rest of the rubbish.

This chapter shows how you can get more for your money by cooking cleverly. You can still buy those offers but just make sure you use them all, or make two batches of your dish and freeze one for later. These recipes use fruit and vegetables that we all buy (no obscure or unprounceable ingredients here), but have perhaps run out of ideas as to what to do with them, so feeling uninspired they go off and go to waste. We all buy fresh fruit and vegetables on a regular basis and as these are some of the cheapest

ingredients, particularly when in season, they are essential to cooking on a shoestring and produce we should maximise to its full potential. So try making Toffee Apples using only a handful of basic ingredients that you should have to hand (see page 142), or preserve your purchases by making Homemade Pickled Vegetables (see page 136) to stock up your storecupboard or use those limp carrots to bake up a batch of Carrot Cookies (see page 152).

Nearly all of the vegetable dishes in this chapter could be served as a main meal, meaning that you can save money a few times a week by not buying expensive ingredients such as meat or fish. Not only good for your wallet but good for your health too as studies have linked a meat-heavy diet to heart disease, cancer and stroke. Using up the veg you have is a guaranteed way to make a healthy and cheap dinner.

So get savvy with your shopping, be aware of which fruits and vegetables are in season as invariably gluts of these will resort in good offers from shops and supermarkets, and get inventive with the ingredients that you have to hand.

Broad Bean, Feta and Courgette Salad

This simple, extremely colourful and summery dish can be served in so many different ways. As it is, it is perfect, and leftovers are delicious served with grilled white fish, or stirred through cooked pasta for a quick lunch, or even mixed into a risotto.

Preparation 15 minutes (longer if you're going to pod the broad beans), plus marinating
Serves 2–3, with lunch sorted the next day

salt

3 large courgettes, cut into ribbons

zest and juice of 2 lemons

50ml extra virgin olive oil

250g broad beans or peas (use fresh if in season, if not frozen ones, defrosted, are fine)

3 spring onions, finely sliced

1 red chilli, finely chopped

150g feta cheese

30g fresh mint leaves

To serve (optional)

crusty bread

1 Put a pan of water on the hob, throw in a large pinch of salt and bring to the boil. Put the courgette ribbons into a mixing bowl and add the lemon juice (but reserve the zest), half the olive oil and a pinch of salt. Leave these to marinate for 20 minutes while you prepare all the other ingredients.

2 Cook the broad beans for 30 seconds in the boiling water, then drain and refresh in cold water.

3 Once the courgettes have marinated add the spring onions, chilli and the cooked broad beans to the bowl with the courgettes. Pile onto a platter. Pour over all the juices that are in the bottom of the bowl as well. Crumble over the feta and the fresh mint leaves. Drizzle with the remaining olive oil and sprinkle over the lemon zest. Serve with crusty bread and a little more olive oil on the side.

TIP All these ingredients will make an amazing chilled soup. Simply blitz all the ingredients (minus the feta) with 300ml vegetable stock and chill well before serving with the feta crumbled on top.

Courgette Rösti, grilled Mushroom and Poached Egg

I've said it before and this won't be the last time I say it — I LOVE to eat breakfast for dinner. Let me explain why. It generally takes me a little while to get into the swing of things in the morning — it's always a bit chaotic, the phone never stops and I have emails coming out of my ears! I never have time for a really good meal. I generally eat a big breakfast only at the weekend when my brain doesn't need to function at such a high speed and I can kick back and relax a little. Therefore, I tend to miss out on my favourite meal of the day during the week, so I've learned how to make breakfasts fit for an evening meal. Here's one of them.

Preparation 10 minutes
Cooking 25–30 minutes
Serves 2

200g waxy potatoes
1 large courgette or 2 small (about 100g)
salt and freshly ground black pepper
2 medium eggs and 1 egg yolk
4 tablespoons plain flour
3 tablespoons olive oil, plus extra for drizzling
2 large flat mushrooms (any mushroom will do, however)
2 garlic cloves, grated or sliced

To serve (optional)
grilled tomatoes
a handful of watercress

1 First, you need to make the rösti. Peel the potatoes, then put a grater on a very clean tea towel and grate the potatoes using the largest side with the biggest holes. Do the same with the courgette, but there's no need to peel this. Pick up each corner of the tea towel and squeeze the potato and courgette mixture into the sink or a bowl to remove all the excess liquid. If you don't do this, the rösti may fall apart while cooking.

2 Tip the squeezed potato and courgette mixture into a bowl, season with salt and pepper, add one egg yolk and the flour, then mix well and shape into two patties approximately 1–1.5cm high. Put a frying pan on the hob, set the heat to medium and add the olive oil. When hot, carefully lay in the röstis and cook for 6–8 minutes per side. Control the heat, as you don't want them to over-colour. Keep them warm while you cook the eggs and mushrooms.

3 Preheat the grill to high. Peel the mushrooms and put them on the grill pan. Drizzle with oil, scatter over the garlic and season with salt and pepper. Put under the hot grill and cook for 4–5 minutes per side. If serving grilled tomatoes with this dish, cook those at the same time.

4 Finally, poach the eggs (see page 159, step 1 for instructions). Serve the röstis on a large plate, top with a mushroom and lastly the perfectly poached oozy egg. Accompany with grilled tomato and watercress if you wish.

TIP Did you know you can freeze egg whites? Make sure you label how many you are freezing and when you have enough, you can use them to make the perfect mini meringues.

Panzanella

You could always just make breadcrumbs with your stale bread, but why not try this fresh and vibrant Italian salad instead? A baguette, ciabatta, focaccia or country loaf all work well for this recipe, so you should be able to use up one you have to hand.

Serves 4
Preparation 15 minutes, plus marinating

about 2 tablespoons olive oil
1 small stale loaf of bread
1 small cucumber, deseeded and cut into
1cm pieces
2 red peppers, deseeded and cut into
1cm pieces
½ red onion, finely diced
4 plum tomatoes, roughly chopped
1½ tablespoons small capers
in vinegar, drained
20 fresh basil leaves
salt and freshly ground black pepper

For the dressing
2 garlic cloves, crushed
5 tablespoons olive oil
3 tablespoons red wine vinegar (white wine or
balsamic will also work)

1 Heat a large frying pan and add the olive oil. Roughly tear the bread into 1–2cm pieces and fry in the olive oil for about 10 minutes or until it is golden brown. Add a little more oil if you need to.

2 Remove the golden brown croutons from the pan, put them in a large bowl and mix in all the chopped vegetables and capers. Tear in the basil. Season with salt and pepper.

3 Combine the dressing ingredients and pour over the salad.

4 Leave to marinate for as long as possible – at least 20 minutes, but overnight is best (if marinating overnight, cover well and put in the fridge). Serve at room temperature either as a starter or alongside some grilled fish.

Indian-style Spiced Potatoes

I often cook this dish as a vegetarian option when making a curry, but it's also a clever way of using up roast or boiled potatoes and it creates a quick lunch or side dish to go with dinner. If I don't have any leftovers handy I tend to use new potatoes cut in half, but larger ones are fine, although you may find they break up a little more while cooking. I would serve this dish with some warm naan or a few poppadoms and some cool minted yogurt.

Preparation 10 minutes
Cooking 25 minutes
Serves 4

500g unpeeled potatoes, cut into 3cm chunks

salt and freshly ground black pepper

1 tablespoon of Indian Curry Paste

(see page 122)

(if you haven't made the curry paste use:

4cm piece of fresh ginger, peeled

3 large garlic cloves, peeled, 1 large onion,

cut into evenly sized pieces, 1 large red chilli,

2 teaspoons turmeric, 2 teaspoons ground

cumin)

3 tablespoons vegetable oil

4 tomatoes, cut into 2cm pieces

(200g canned tomatoes will also work)

350g spinach (frozen is fine)

30g fresh coriander leaves, roughly chopped

1 Cook the potatoes, until tender in boiling salted water. Drain and leave to cool.

2 If you don't have any Indian Curry Paste already made up, make a paste by combining the ginger, garlic, onion, chilli, turmeric and cumin in a food processor. Blend until you have a coarse paste.

3 Pour the vegetable oil into a large sauté pan and turn the heat to high. Add the paste and move it around the pan using a wooden spoon or silicone spatula for 4–5 minutes. Reduce the heat if you are worried the paste might burn.

4 Add the tomatoes, reduce the heat and simmer for another 5 minutes before adding the potatoes. Heat through before adding the spinach and coriander and allowing it to wilt. Season with salt and pepper, mix well and serve once the spinach is cooked.

TIP If you have any leftover lamb, try shredding it well and mixing it through the potatoes. If you have made a little bit too much of this dish, whisk some eggs into your leftovers and make a spicy frittata (see page 162 for a similar method).

Patatas Bravas

This dish translates as 'brave potatoes' — a name that might be inspired by the spicy kick. It's perfect served with cold meats, olives, chorizo, prawns or any other lovely tapas-style dishes you fancy. I often have it cold for lunch with a salad. I tend to cook this recipe when I need to use up any leftover potatoes. I usually make mine using new potatoes cut in half, as I always have a few handfuls rolling around the bottom of my dry stores, but large baking potatoes cut into 2.5cm chunks, or even leftover roast potatoes also work really well.

Preparation 10 minutes
Cooking 25 minutes
Serves 6

800g new potatoes cut in half (or use large potatoes, peeled and cut into 2.5cm chunks)
1 tablespoon olive oil
salt and freshly ground black pepper

For the sauce
½ tablespoon olive oil
1 onion, diced
1 medium red chilli, chopped
2 garlic cloves, sliced
2 teaspoons sweet paprika (you can also use hot or smoked)
pinch of sugar
1 tablespoon tomato purée
1 x 400g can chopped tomatoes

To serve (optional)
freshly chopped parsley leaves

1 Preheat the oven to 200°C/Gas 6. Put the potatoes on a baking tray. Drizzle with oil, coat well and season with salt and pepper, then cook in the preheated oven for about 25–30 minutes until they are tender and golden brown. Give the baking tray a shake halfway through cooking.

2 While the potatoes are cooking, make the Bravas sauce. Pour the oil into a saucepan and add the onion, chilli and garlic. Add a pinch of salt and cook over a low heat for 10 minutes until the onion is soft and translucent.

3 Now add the paprika, sugar, tomato purée and canned tomatoes. Simmer for about 20 minutes making sure you stir the sauce every couple of minutes to ensure that it's not catching on the bottom of the pan.

4 Serve the potatoes in a bowl and pour over the sauce. Sprinkle with parsley before you serve, if using.

TIP If you have any vegetables left over from the Spanish-style Roast Chicken on page 48, mix these through the potatoes 5 minutes before they are cooked.

Spiced Red Cabbage with Ginger and Apple

I love to eat this dish with roast pork — my favourite is slow-roasted belly or shoulder (follow the instructions for Slow-cooked Roasted Pork Belly with Apples on page 34). This dish is also lovely with some really meaty sausages and a large spoonful of mashed potatoes.

Preparation 15 minutes
Cooking 2 hours
Serves 6

1 medium red cabbage, very finely sliced
1 teaspoon ground cinnamon or
1 cinnamon stick
3 eating or 2 cooking apples, peeled
and grated
3 pieces stem ginger, finely chopped
1 teaspoon ground ginger
5 tablespoons brown sugar
4 tablespoons red wine or balsamic vinegar
about 100ml red wine or apple (optional)
salt and freshly ground black pepper
25g butter

1 Preheat the oven to 180°C/Gas 4. In a medium flameproof casserole with a tight-fitting lid, put all the ingredients except the butter, and mix together well. Season with salt and pepper. Dot the ingredients with butter, put on a round of greaseproof paper and put on the lid.

2 Transfer to the oven and cook for 2 hours. (Alternatively, if you want to speed up the process, this can be cooked on top of the hob. Simply add 200ml red wine and 200ml apple juice and simmer for about 45 minutes until all the juice has evaporated and the cabbage is tender.) Once cooked, the cabbage can be stored for up to a week in an airtight container and the flavour will keep on improving.

TIP If you don't usually buy stem ginger, but now have half a jar of it, go to page 86 and try my Tray-baked Ginger-glazed Salmon.

Homemade Pickled Vegetables

No matter how hard we all try to not waste, occasionally we just can't help but have a few bits left over. Instead of throwing your excess or past-its-best veg away, why not try pickling it? The pickling process preserves your vegetables for months if stored correctly. Pickled vegetables are fantastic served with cheese, cold meats or simply as pre-dinner nibbles with olives and pretzels. So you can take advantage of that buy-one-get-one-free offer in the knowledge that whatever you got for free won't go to waste.

Preparation 20 minutes
Cooking 8 minutes, plus cooling
Makes 2–3 medium-sized Kilner jars, about 1.5 litres

450ml white wine or cider vinegar
100g caster sugar
5cm piece of fresh ginger, peeled and cut into fine matchsticks
2 bay leaves
6–8 whole peppercorns
1 teaspoon salt
150g cauliflower, cut into small florets
150g green beans, cut into 2cm pieces
2 small carrots (or 1 large), peeled and cut into 1cm x 3cm matchsticks or diced
100g seedless grapes
150g cucumber, deseeded and cut into 1cm dice

1 Pour the vinegar into a saucepan with 300ml water. Add the sugar, ginger, bay leaves, peppercorns and salt and bring to the boil. Add the vegetables and grapes to the pan and simmer for 2–3 minutes before removing from the heat and pouring the entire contents of the pan into a non-metallic bowl. Leave to cool completely.

2 Once cooled, divide the vegetables and the liquor between the sterilised jars, seal well and store for later use. I would recommend leaving the vegetables to marinate for at least a week before using.

TIP To sterilise the jars, either boil them in clean water or simple put them into the dishwasher on the highest setting. You can make this recipe with pretty much any vegetables or hard fruit you wish so please don't feel you have to sick to my recommendations.

Minted Berries

If you do happen to come across a berry bargain in your local supermarket when they are in season, even if the berries are looking a little the worse for wear, do buy them. They can be either frozen and stored for the next time you want a summer pudding, marinated and served with some delicious vanilla ice cream, or topped with some tasty Storecupboard Granola from page 120. If you have some left over blitz with a couple of tablespoons of yogurt and half a banana for a smoothie. Any berries will work for this recipe, but I like strawberries best.

**Preparation 5 minutes,
plus marinating
Serves 4**

zest and juice of 2 lemons
2 tablespoons caster sugar
3–4 tablespoons crème de cassis, limoncello
or any other fruity liqueur – Ribena works well
if cooking for kids (optional)
20 fresh mint leaves, shredded
500g berries

TIP This is also great
served in champagne flutes
and topped with bubbles if
it's a special occasion.

1 In a large bowl, mix the lemon juice and zest, the caster sugar, liqueur (if using), and the shredded mint.

2 If you are using strawberries, core them. Wash the berries well before mixing with the marinade. Leave to soak for at least 30 minutes, or preferably overnight, at room temperature before serving.

Elderflower Jelly with Lime Granita

This is such an elegant little dessert that it never fails to please even the most difficult diners. As long as you have some sort of cordial, a bit of zest, a few leaves of gelatine and running water, you'll have all you need to make this delicious dessert.

Preparation 15 minutes
Setting and chilling 3–4 hours
Serves 6

For the jellies
4 gelatine leaves
about 150ml elderflower cordial (or any cordial you have, summer fruits is nice)
450ml water (if it's a special occasion, cava or prosecco is a nice alternative)

For the granita
100ml elderflower cordial
350ml water
zest and juice of 3 limes

To serve
10 fresh leaves mint, shredded

1 You can do this any way round you like, but I prefer to start with the jellies. Soak the gelatine in a little cold water (just enough to cover the leaves) for 15 minutes until soft.

2 Heat the elderflower cordial in a saucepan and, when the gelatine is soft, pour it along with the water into the warmed elderflower. Heat until the gelatine has completely dissolved. Taste the mixture at this stage – you may want it a little sweeter and, if so, add another splash of elderflower cordial.

3 Now pour the mixture into your desired serving glasses (I like to use old-fashioned champagne flutes). Put the jellies in the fridge to chill and set while you make the granita.

4 Combine all the ingredients for the granita and pour into a plastic container that fits in the freezer. Put in a freezer drawer. Stir the granita with a fork every 20 minutes or so over the next 2 hours to ensure it doesn't set hard. Once the jellies are set, the granita will be ready.

5 Serve the jellies with a large scoop of the granita and garnish with a little shredded mint.

TIP If you want to make this in advance you can. You will simply need to remove the granita from its container and blend it in a food processor to break up the ice crystals before re-freezing for 30 minutes or so and serving.

Toffee Apples

You really should give this recipe a go as we all need a nostalgic taste of our childhoods once in a while. These are great fun to make and a fraction of the price of shop-bought toffee apples. Just watch your teeth!

Preparation 5 minutes
Cooking 15 minutes
Setting 15 minutes
Serves 6

225g caster sugar
110ml water
a drop of white or cider vinegar
25g butter
2 tablespoons golden syrup
6 small eating apples
(Braeburns work well)

1 Put the sugar and water in a small saucepan set over a medium heat. Allow the sugar to melt before adding the vinegar, butter and the golden syrup and bringing to the boil. Don't stir it at this stage. You want to get the toffee to hard-crack stage, so that when you add a tiny drop of the cooked toffee to a bowl of cold water, it instantly forms into a hard ball. The temperature for this is 135–140°C. It should take about 10 minutes from boiling point to reach this stage.

2 Line a baking tray with greaseproof paper. Skewer each apple at the bottom end with a wooden stick, wooden skewer or lolly stick. When the toffee is ready, tilt the pan so that the toffee collects at one side. Dip each apple into the hot mixture and coat it evenly in the toffee.

3 Put the toffee apples on the lined baking tray with the stick end pointing up and allow the toffee to set for 15 minutes. If you want to eat the apples a day or so later, wrap them in cellophane and secure it in place with string or a pretty ribbon.

TIP Small apples work best for this, but do use whatever you have to hand. For a variation, try small pears.

Apple Strudel

We're all drawn to the buy-one-get-one-free (or **BOGOF**) offer from time to time. It makes you feel as if you've got a real bargain. The trouble is finding what to do with the six extra apples in your fruit bowl before they go past their best. Apple Strudel is my preferred way of using up the apple glut. If you don't fancy a strudel the week you bought your apples, no problem. Just make it and pop it in the freezer. It will last in there happily for a month or two.

Preparation 15 minutes
Cooking 30–35 minutes
Serves 6

4 eating apples of your choosing, peeled, cored and cut into 1–2cm chunks

100g caster sugar

100g sultanas, raisins or other dried berries

½ teaspoon ground cinnamon

juice and zest of 1 lemon

150g pecan nuts or walnuts (optional)

75g butter

6 sheets of filo pastry (about 30 x 20cm)

1 tablespoon icing sugar or brown granulated sugar

To serve (optional)

vanilla ice cream

1 Preheat the oven to 180°C/Gas 4. Put the apples into a large heavy saucepan with the sugar, dried fruits, cinnamon, lemon juice and zest. Cook over a medium heat, allowing the apples to gently cook down and slightly break up. This will take about 10 minutes. (You can also add a splash of booze at this stage, if you wish – I find a dash of brandy works very well.) Once you are happy with the texture of the apples, add the pecan nuts or walnuts, if using, and leave the mixture to cool completely.

2 Melt the butter in a small saucepan. Lay out the first filo sheet on a board in front of you and brush it generously with melted butter. Lay another sheet on top and repeat the process. Repeat with the remaining sheets of pastry and brush the final layer with yet more butter. Spoon the cooled apple mixture along the centre of the layered filo stack. Roll the strudel up into a fat sausage, ensuring the seal is at the bottom. Use a palette knife to transfer the strudel onto a baking tray that has been lined with greaseproof paper. Brush the rolled strudel with more melted butter and sprinkle with a little icing sugar or brown granulated sugar for a really crunchy top. If you plan to freeze the strudel, do it at this stage and cover it well with clingfilm, otherwise bake for 35–40 minutes until golden brown. Slice and serve while hot with vanilla ice cream, if you wish.

TIPS Buy your apples when in season to guarantee the best flavour and price and try to buy your pastry from a Turkish or Greek shop or market if you are lucky enough to have one close by. It will be slightly cheaper than buying it from a supermarket and is often of a far better quality.

If you fancy
a change then
pears also work
well in place
of the apples.

Peaches-and-cream Panna Cotta

I make this recipe when I really don't have time for any fussing around. Since I generally have a pretty well-stocked storecupboard, I never need to shop for any of these ingredients and this dessert can be thrown together in minutes. The end result is always a hit.

Preparation 15 minutes
Setting 4 hours
Makes 8 espresso-cup-sized desserts

3 gelatine leaves
400g canned peaches in natural juice, drained
but liquor reserved
(or use soft fresh peaches, peeled)
100ml milk
200ml double cream
2 drops vanilla extract or 1 teaspoon vanilla
bean paste (optional)
3 tablespoons caster sugar

1 Soak the gelatine leaves in a little cold water. Put the peaches with half the liquor into a blender and blend to a smooth purée.

2 Heat the milk and double cream with the vanilla and sugar and bring to just below boiling point. Ensure all the sugar has dissolved before taking the pan off the heat.

3 Remove the soaked gelatine from the water and squeeze out any excess water. Put the soaked gelatine into the hot cream and stir well.

4 Spoon 2 teaspoons of the peach purée into the bottom of each espresso cup. Allow the cream to cool slightly before stirring in the remaining peach purée. Carefully fill the cups with the peach-flavoured cream and put into the fridge to set.

5 Serve once set, with a biscotti if you like.

Frangipan and Apricot Clafoutis

This clafoutis is one of the easiest desserts to make and uses very few ingredients. Traditionally a clafoutis is made using cherries, and if you have some by all means please use them. However, I often use canned fruits to make desserts. They are already cooked so no need for poaching first and they can be picked up for a very reasonable price. Best of all is that they don't go off, so are perfect for a last-minute pudding. This is a bit of a cheat clafoutis, but it still tastes wonderful.

Preparation 10 minutes
Cooking 35–40 minutes
Serves 4

100g caster sugar
100g softened butter
100g ground almonds
3 large eggs
a drop of vanilla extract
zest of 1 orange or lemon
1 x 400g can halved apricots, drained
icing sugar

To serve
fresh cream

1 Preheat the oven to 180°C/Gas 4. Mix together the sugar, butter and ground almonds, either by hand or in a food processor. Add the eggs one at a time along with the vanilla extract and the orange or lemon zest. The batter should look quite thick.

2 Arrange half the apricots in the bottom of a 20 x 15cm baking dish before spooning over the batter. Dot the batter with the remaining apricots, sliced-side up, and dust with icing sugar. Put on a baking tray and cook for 35–40 minutes.

3 Once cooked, the dessert should be golden brown and completely set. Remove from the oven, dust with a little more icing sugar and serve with fresh cream.

TIP This recipe can be made using almost any canned fruit. If you don't have that, try dotting the clafoutis mixture with a few dollops of jam before baking — it works just as well.

French Toast with Plum Compote

I don't need to explain to you why French toast is such a brilliant recipe, but I may have to explain why I have chosen to pair it with plum compote. Come late early autumn, my garden is slightly obscured by the most magnificent plum tree (which actually belongs to my neighbours next door), but its branches, laden with fruit, croop perfectly over my fence and they are just desperate to be picked. I have made jam, crumbles, chutneys and salads, but this dish has to be my all-time favourite way of using plums. If you don't have access to a plum tree, buy your fruit when in season. You'll get far more for your money and it will taste so much sweeter.

Preparation 10 minutes
Cooking 25 minutes
Serves 4

3 medium eggs, beaten
100ml milk
½ teaspoon ground cinnamon
8 slices day-old white bread, croissant or brioche
(I like to use a rustic country loaf)
2 tablespoons vegetable oil
25g butter
2 tablespoons icing sugar

For the compote
400g plums, stone removed and cut into eighths
4 tablespoons brown sugar
juice of ½ lemon
2 tablespoons water
1 cinnamon stick or 1 star anise

1 To make the plum compote put the plum slices in a saucepan with the sugar, lemon juice, water and the cinnamon or star anise. Allow the plums to simmer over a low heat until they start to break down. Check for sweetness – you may need a touch more sugar, depending on the ripeness of the plums.

2 Beat the eggs with the milk and the ground cinnamon and soak the slices of bread in the mixture. Put a large frying pan on the hob over a high heat. Add the oil and lay in the slices of soaked bread – you may need to do this in batches. Once the bread starts to colour and turn golden brown, turn it over before adding a little butter. Once you are happy with the colour, remove the French toast from the pan, put onto serving plates and dust with icing sugar.

3 When the plums have broken down slightly spoon them generously over the French toast and serve.

TIP If you want to make extra compote, do this and store it in a Kilner jar or airtight container. It works really well on your porridge in the mornings or spooned over yogurt.

Carrot Cookies

Ever wondered what to do with those few poor, slightly floppy carrots that are hanging about in the bottom of your vegetable tray? Well, here you go. An old wartime classic that, as far as I'm concerned, will never go out of fashion. A brilliant way to get a bit of vitamin C into your kids and one of your five a day.

Preparation 10 minutes
Cooking 12 minutes,
plus cooling
Makes 10–12

85g butter or margarine
130g sugar
130g plain flour
½ teaspoon baking powder
2 small carrots (or 1 large), peeled and grated
1 teaspoon ground cinnamon

1 Preheat the oven to 180°C/Gas 4. Put the butter and sugar in a food processor and cream together until pale and fluffy. Add the flour and baking powder. Add the grated carrot and the cinnamon and blend again. If the mixture is looking a bit dry, add a tablespoon of water.

2 Divide the mixture into balls, each measuring about 3cm in circumference, and put these onto a baking tray lined with greaseproof paper. Bake in the preheated oven for 10–12 minutes until golden brown.

Peanut Butter and Banana Cake

This recipe will also give you fantastic muffins. Follow it in exactly the same way, only when the mix is ready, simply spoon it into silicone muffin cases rather than a cake tin

**Preparation 15 minutes
Cooking 40 minutes,
plus cooling
Makes 12 squares**

200g butter, at room temperature
200g sugar (brown is best for a more
caramel-like flavour)
6 tablespoons crunchy, salted peanut butter
3 medium eggs
100ml milk
250g plain flour, sifted
½ teaspoon baking powder
2 ripe bananas, squashed using
the back of a fork

1 Preheat the oven to 180°C/Gas 4. Line a 20 x 20cm square cake tin with greaseproof paper.

2 Cream the butter and sugar together until you have a smooth and light paste. Add the peanut butter and mix again before adding the eggs, one by one, whisking all the time, followed by the milk. Now fold in the sifted flour, baking powder and, finally, the squashed bananas. Spoon the mixture into the lined cake tin and cook for 35–40 minutes. You want the sponge to be just cooked and golden brown on top – insert a skewer into the centre if you're unsure, if it comes out clean, the cake is ready.

3 Allow to cool before cutting into 12 squares and serving with a lovely cup of tea.

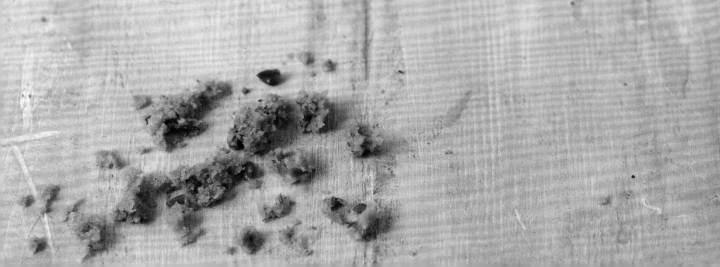

Eggs and Dairy

Eggs and Dairy

As long as you have eggs on the kitchen counter or in the fridge at home you can always eat well. If I'm cooking for myself or just don't fancy another meat-loaded dinner, I will rustle up something using a few eggs, salt and pepper and a handful of other ingredients that will leave me extremely satisfied and very full (with no need for any shopping). Eggs are a brilliant source of protein, so fantastic for kids, as well as high in vitamins B and D, in addition to being a fantastically affordable and versatile ingredient.

So why not make a simple Potato and Caramelised Onion Tortillla (see page 162)? Delicious, and doubly so if you have made a large one with enough going spare for wonderful cold lunch with a big crispy salad the next day. Or a tasty Poached Egg and Crispy Bacon Salad (see page 159) with bitter leaves, as a variation on the traditional combination of bacon and eggs. If you are really hungry, you can serve it with a chunk of crusty bread on the side to mop up all those sticky, rich dribbles of egg yolk. And if you don't fancy washing up then One-pan Spicy Eggs (see page 160) requires just that.

If you have a recipe that requires just the yolks, never throw away the whites, these can be frozen, ready for the next time you need the whip up a meringue. Just remember to label the container or bag with how many egg whites are inside. Yolks can also be frozen ready for the next batch of crème brûlée or lemon tart.

Dairy products are not just available to put in your tea or coffee. Full-fat milk or crème fraîche (providing you don't boil the crème fraîche) can be used in most puddings where double cream is required, unless you need it for whipping, so there's no need to rush out and spend money just because you don't have enough of an ingredient to finish off your custard. It is also a good idea to use half milk, half cream, on the odd occasion for a less rich dessert. Dairy is not an expensive ingredient and can elevate a meal from good to luxurious with a simple splash or two. So as well as forming the basis of these recipes try adding it others throughout the book – a spoonful of crème fraîche makes a lovely additionto a soup or pasta dish such as Sausage Meatball Carbonara (see page 98).

Poached Egg and Crispy Bacon Salad

This is one of my all-time favourite salads. It takes only ten minutes to prepare and uses ingredients that you're bound to have in the fridge and cupboards, so there's usually no shopping required.

Preparation 10 minutes
Cooking 25 minutes
Serves 4

4 eggs
2 tablespoons olive oil
2 red onions, finely chopped
salt and freshly ground black pepper
150g smoked lardons, diced, or smoked
bacon, cut into small pieces
2 large garlic cloves, peeled and squashed
(but not chopped)
75g stale bread, cut or torn into 1cm pieces
1 large bag of mixed-leaf salad
(or 4 heads of endive)

For the dressing
2 teaspoons Dijon mustard
1 teaspoon clear honey
1 tablespoon balsamic vinegar
2 tablespoons olive oil
a freshly grated pinch of nutmeg (optional)

1 Put a large saucepan of water on the hob over a high heat. Bring the water to the boil, then turn the heat right down so the water is just below boiling point. Crack the eggs into four small ramekins. Take a whisk and stir the water to create a vortex. When the vortex has started to slow down, pour the eggs into the centre, one at a time very gently. Poach the eggs gently for 3½ minutes. Don't be tempted to touch them! Don't season the water, as this will encourage the egg to break down. When each egg has had its poaching time, remove it using a slotted spoon and put onto absorbent kitchen paper to drain while you make the rest of the dish.

2 Meanwhile, put a large frying pan on the hob and turn the heat to medium. Add 1 tablespoon of the olive oil, then the diced onions. Cook with a pinch of salt for 5–6 minutes until they start to turn sweet and translucent. Turn up the heat and add the diced lardons or bacon and the squashed garlic cloves. Allow to cook until the lardons turn golden brown and the fat of the lardons has started to melt – this should take about 6 minutes. When you are happy with the colour, remove the lardons and onions and drain on some kitchen paper. Leave the fat and any crispy bits in the pan along with the garlic.

3 Add the remaining olive oil to the pan and the bread. Season with salt and pepper, and fry for 4–5 minutes until the bread is golden brown and has soaked up all the oil. Turn off the heat.

4 Make the dressing by combining the mustard, honey and balsamic vinegar in a bowl before slowly adding the oil. Add the nutmeg, if using, and season to taste

5 Put the cooked onions, and croutons into a large salad bowl and add the leaves. Pour over half of the dressing. Portion out the salad between four plates. Put a poached egg on top of each one and add a final drizzle of the dressing.

One-pan Spicy Eggs

A classic midweek dish... it ticks all the boxes — healthy, quick to prepare, quick to cook, minimal shopping, reasonably priced ingredients and extremely satisfying to eat. Breakfast, lunch or dinner — this dish is a winner.

Preparation 10 minutes
Cooking 15 minutes
Serves 2

2 tablespoons vegetable oil
2 garlic cloves, finely chopped
2 spring onions, finely sliced
2 teaspoons ground cumin, plus extra for sprinkling
1 teaspoon ground coriander
½ teaspoon hot chilli powder
pinch of sugar
200g cherry tomatoes, halved or plum tomatoes, deseeded and quartered
4 medium eggs
2 flatbreads
35g freshly chopped coriander leaves

For the mint yogurt (optional)
35g freshly chopped coriander or mint leaves
150g fat-free natural or Greek yogurt
½ teaspoon ground cumin
juice of ½ lemon

1 To make the mint yogurt, mix the chopped mint or coriander together with the yogurt, cumin and the lemon juice. Set aside.

2 Put a large non-stick pan over a low heat and add the vegetable oil. Add the garlic to the pan along with the spring onions and cook for 2–3 minutes, stirring all the time so that the garlic doesn't burn. Add the spices and sugar and stir well. Next, add the tomatoes. Coat them in the spices and cook until soft but not mushy – 5 minutes is plenty. Make four gaps in the tomato mixture and crack in the eggs. Season the top of each egg with a small pinch of cumin and a little salt. Cook until the whites are firm but the yolk is runny. I often pop the pan under the grill if the whites are taking a little while to cook.

3 While this is happening, grill the flatbreads until warm and a little crispy at the edges. Once the egg and tomato dish is ready, you can either take the pan straight to the table or scoop it out and serve it piled onto the grilled flatbreads. Scatter over the fresh coriander and serve with the yogurt on the side.

Potato and Caramelised Onion Tortilla

There is no end to the amount of ingredients that you can add to a tortilla or Spanish omelette. It is a fantastic dish to make if you are trying to use up some leftovers, as it can be adapted any way you choose. This recipe will give you the foundations for what I class as a great tortilla, using potatoes and onions. What you add to it next, if anything, is your choice — tomatoes, peppers, cooked vegetables, bacon or prawns all work well.

Preparation 10 minutes
Cooking 30 minutes
Serves 4

3 large potatoes (about 600g), peeled and
sliced into 2mm thick slices
3 large white onions, peeled and thinly sliced
2 tablespoons olive oil
salt and freshly ground black pepper
10–12 large eggs
smoked paprika (optional)

To serve (optional)
green salad
Patatas Bravas Sauce
(see page 134)

1 Start by steaming the potato slices. This can be done either in a proper steamer basket, if you have one, or you can improvise by placing a small colander inside a big saucepan that is filled halfway with water, then put on a tight-fitting lid. Cook for 12 minutes from boiling, or until the potatoes are tender but not falling apart.

2 While the potatoes are steaming, put the onions into a 24cm non-stick frying pan with the olive oil. Add a pinch of salt and allow to cook for 15 minutes over a low heat. Keep moving the onions around the pan so that they cook evenly and don't over-colour.

3 Preheat the grill to medium. Once the potatoes are cooked, lay them into the frying pan evenly with the onions. Season well with salt and pepper as you go. Whisk the eggs in a large bowl and pour them over the potatoes and onions. Sprinkle over the smoked paprika, if using, and allow to cook for 10 minutes over a low heat before transferring the pan to the grill for a further 6–8 minutes. When the eggs are set, the tortilla is ready. To serve, gently slide the tortilla onto a board and serve with green salad and Patatas Bravas sauce if you wish.

TIP This dish is great cold and will make a delicious lunchbox filler or portable picnic treat.

Try these with my Patatas
Bravas recipe (see page 134).

Chocolate Spread Bread and Butter Pudding

I try to have everything I need for at least one or two good old-fashioned puddings that can be whipped together in minutes without the need for me to have to go to the shops. This chocolate bread and butter dessert is no exception to the rule. If you fancy making this slightly richer and more indulgent replace the milk with double cream.

Preparation 15 minutes, plus soaking
Cooking 30 minutes
Serves 6

75g softened butter, plus extra for greasing and dotting on top
400g brioche, croissants, pain au chocolat or Madeira cake (a few days old is fine)
75g chocolate spread
550ml whole milk (or half milk and half double cream, if you want to be more indulgent)
175g caster sugar, plus 1 tablespoon for the top (if you make your own vanilla sugar, use this instead)
2 drops vanilla extract
2 large eggs

To serve
custard

1 Preheat the oven to 180°C/Gas 4. Grease a 1 litre ovenproof dish with a little butter. Cut your chosen bread into 1.5cm slices (or simply in half, if using croissants). Spread each slice (front and back) generously with the softened butter, followed by the chocolate spread.

2 Lay the buttered slices into the ovenproof dish. Don't worry if some bits stick up and are at angles – that will make the overall dish more attractive and rustic looking. Pour the milk, sugar and vanilla into a small saucepan and heat slightly to dissolve the sugar. Whisk the eggs in a separate bowl. Once the milk is hot, pour it over the eggs, whisking as you do so. Pour the mixture over the layered bread and leave to soak for 20 minutes.

3 Sprinkle the top with a little caster sugar and dot with 5–6 small pieces of butter. Bake for 25–30 minutes.

4 Serve hot, with custard.

Apricot Jam and Cinnamon Swirls

If you happen to have a packet of puff pastry hanging around in the back of the freezer that needs using, I seriously urge you to give these a go. They are perfect for little teatime treats or as an after-school snack for the kids... or mum.

Preparation 10 minutes, plus resting
Cooking 20 minutes
Makes 16 swirls

375g puff pastry, ready rolled or rolled into a rectangle about 2mm thick (these are also great made using bun dough)
4 large tablespoons chunky apricot jam (if you have any leftover dried apricots from the Lamb Shoulder Shank Tagine on page 26, chop them up and throw those in as well as any chopped nuts you might have)
1 heaped teaspoon ground cinnamon, plus extra for dusting
1 egg, beaten
1 tablespoon icing sugar, for dusting

1 Roll out the puff pastry and lay it in front of you. Spread the jam over and then liberally scatter over any chopped apricots or nuts, if you have them. Now add the cinnamon – I tend to do this pinch by pinch so that it's as evenly distributed as possible or, of course, you can use a sugar sifter or tea strainer.

2 Now roll the pastry as tightly as you can to make a long sausage. Cut the sausage into 16 pieces, each about 1.5cm thick, and lay these onto a greased or lined baking tray. Press them down slightly to make them flatter and rounder. Brush them with the beaten egg and put into the fridge for 15 minutes to set. Preheat the oven to 200°C/Gas 6.

3 Remove the swirls from the fridge and cook in the preheated oven for 20 minutes until golden brown.

4 Mix the extra cinnamon with the icing sugar and dust the swirls while still warm using a tea strainer or fine sieve. Serve just as they are with a cup of tea or with vanilla ice cream.

 TIP These can be made with any jam – strawberry, raspberry or even with marmalade. They also work well with golden syrup or honey.

Honeycomb and Caramel Parfait

Parfait is basically a posh word for a block of ice cream made in a loaf tin. It's super-quick and really cheap to make. I am Crunchie-bar crazy so I always bash up a couple and fold the crumbs through my parfait, but Maltesers or even M&Ms work a treat. This is a brilliant dinner party dish if you are watching the pennies, as it looks really impressive.

Preparation 10 minutes
Freezing minimum 3 hours
Serves 8

115g butter
110g caster or soft brown sugar
200g condensed milk
150ml milk
300ml double cream
2 Crunchie bars (or your favourite chocolate bar), roughly chopped into small pieces
berries, to decorate (optional)

1 Put the butter and sugar in a non-stick saucepan set over a low heat. Stir until the butter melts and the sugar dissolves. Add the condensed milk, bring to the boil and stir until the mixture turns golden brown. Stir in the milk very carefully, as the hot mixture may splutter when the cold liquid is added. Leave to cool.

2 Whisk the double cream to firm peaks and fold into the cooled condensed milk mixture along with the chocolate pieces.

3 Double-line a 900g loaf tin with clingfilm and pour in the mixture. Cover the top with another piece of clingfilm and put the tin into the freezer until the parfait is set and frozen.

4 To serve, run a knife around the edge of the loaf tin or, alternatively, dip the bottom of the tin into boiling water for a few seconds to help release the parfait from the tin. Turn out the parfait onto a board and cut it into 1.5cm slices. Decorate with a few berries before you serve if you wish.

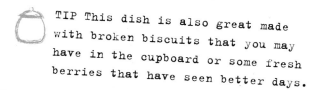

TIP This dish is also great made with broken biscuits that you may have in the cupboard or some fresh berries that have seen better days.

Marinades and Sauces

Having a few marinades and sauces in your repertoire is such an important part of day-to-day cooking. Not only will it make your life ten times easier when trying to think of yet another exciting way of jazzing up a chicken leg, but it will also save you a huge amount of time – and money – in the long run and will definitely add a bit of pizzazz to your suppers.

In this little section, you will see a few of my personal favourite marinades and sauces that can all be made in advance. Many of these will help you to use up some of the herbs and spices you buy for one recipe that end up in the salad drawer in the fridge, never to see the light of day again.

For storing marinades and sauces, invest in a few Kilner jars or, if you can't stretch to that, some jam jar covers that you can pop onto sterilised glass jars of your choosing. You can sterilise the jars in some boiling water or in the microwave. As long as the top of your sauce or marinade has a little layer of olive oil on top to stop it oxidising and is in a jar with a tight-fitting lid, it will last in the fridge for a few weeks.

Harissa

Use with lamb, fish, chicken, prawns or halloumi.

Makes 300g

2 tablespoons cumin seeds
1 teaspoon caraway seeds
1 teaspoon coriander seeds
4 tablespoons tomato purée
250g chopped tomatoes, fresh or canned
4 hot chillies, with seeds
3 garlic cloves, peeled
2 shallots, peeled
2 tablespoons olive oil

Dry roast the spices in a frying pan for 3–4 minutes, then grind them to a smooth powder using a pestle and mortar. Blend the tomato purée, chopped tomatoes, chillies, garlic and shallots to a smooth paste in a food processor, then add the spices. Transfer to a pan and simmer for 10 minutes over a very low heat. Pour the contents into the sterilised jar and cover with the olive oil. Seal well. This will keep for up to three months in the fridge.

Indian Curry Paste

This is a really generic paste that I use for many curries.

Makes 200g

1 large red onion, roughly chopped
5cm piece of fresh ginger, peeled and roughly chopped
8 garlic cloves, peeled
2–3 green or red chillies, depending on how hot you like it
1 tablespoon tomato purée
3 teaspoons ground cumin
3 teaspoons ground coriander
2 teaspoons ground turmeric
1 teaspoons ground cinnamon
1 tablespoon ground cloves
2 tablespoons olive oil

Combine all the ingredients except the oil in a food processor and blitz until smooth. Store in an airtight, sterilised contained and cover with the oil to stop it oxidising. This paste will last one month in the fridge. It can also be frozen in ice cube trays if you prefer.

Barbecue Sauce
Makes 350ml

2 tablespoons tomato purée
4 tablespoons tomato ketchup
200ml Coca-Cola
2 tablespoons sweet chilli sauce
1 teaspoon chilli flakes
1 teaspoon ground ginger
3 tablespoons clear honey
2 tablespoons Worcestershire sauce

Combine all the ingredients in a pan and bring to the boil. Simmer for 30 minutes. This will keep for three months in the fridge in an airtight, sterilised jar.

Sticky Asian Sauce

I love this on pork chops but it also makes a great sauce for a stir-fry.

Makes 150ml

5cm piece of fresh ginger, peeled and roughly chopped

4 garlic cloves, roughly chopped

2 red chillies, roughly chopped

1 stalk lemongrass, roughly chopped (optional)

6 tablespoons soy sauce

2 tablespoons sweet chilli sauce

2 teaspoons clear honey

juice and zest of 2 limes

2 teaspoons all spice or Chinese five-spice powder

Blend all the ingredients together in a food processor and bottle it in a sterilised bottle. Perfect for marinating fish, chicken and prawns.

Thai Green Curry Paste

Not only will this make you a fantastic curry but also a brilliant marinade (see page 57 for Thai-style Chicken Wings).

Makes 150g

4 long green chillies

4 garlic cloves, roughly chopped

5cm piece of fresh ginger, peeled and roughly chopped

1 stalk lemongrass, bashed and roughly chopped

juice and zest of 3 limes

6 kaffir limes leaves (dried is fine)

1 large bunch of fresh coriander,

including the stalks

2 tablespoons fish sauce

2 tablespoons olive oil

Start by blending the chillies, garlic, ginger and lemongrass together in a food processor to form a paste. Then add all the remaining ingredients and blitz until smooth. This can be stored for one month in the fridge in a sealed and sterilised container.

Pesto

Pesto is traditionally made with basil, but who says it can't be made with any other herbs? I often make a coriander pesto or use a combination of herbs that need using. Follow my basic quantities below and try a few different combinations: red pepper and walnut, sun-blushed tomato and hazelnuts or coriander and lime. Stir it or spread it – pesto can be used for a whole host of recipes – see Courgette, Pesto and Ravioli Bake on page 95.

Makes 200g

50g toasted pine nuts or hazelnuts, walnuts, pecan nuts or macadamia nuts

50g grated Parmesan cheese (Pecorino also works well)

1 large bunch of fresh basil, (or coriander or parsley)

2 large garlic cloves, chopped or grated

zest and juice 1 lemon

150ml olive oil

Blitz or pound the ingredients in a food processor or pound using a pestle and mortar until you have a textured paste. Store pesto in a sterilised, airtight container in the fridge for up to three weeks.

Chimichurri

This is an Argentinean spicy salsa. It works perfectly with red meat, beef particularly, but is also a brilliant accompaniment or marinade for seafood. I often buy meat when on offer, smother it in this marinade and freeze it. The acidity in the salsa tenderises the meat and makes it super tasty. Try serving with onglet steak or a turkey burger.

Makes 200g

3 long red chillies, finely chopped, seeds in or out, depending on how brave you are

6 garlic cloves, grated

1 large bunch flatleaf parsley, finely chopped

2 tablespoons dried oregano (fresh is even better or I sometimes use fresh coriander)

5 tablespoons red wine vinegar

5 tablespoons olive oil

salt and freshly ground black pepper

Chop everything by hand, mix well and store. Try to wait 24 hours before eating if you can resist the temptation.

Stocks

To make the perfect chicken or vegetable stock

Place the chicken bones into your largest saucepan, along with the giblets, if you have them. Don't add the skin or your stock will become oily. Wash and add your vegetables – I recommend carrots, celery, onions (halved), leeks – and then some garlic, peppercorns and herbs like thyme, rosemary parsley and bay leaves. You can also add mushrooms for a darker, richer stock.

A good chicken stock needs to be about half chicken bones and half vegetables. So, one chicken carcass will need roughly 1 carrot, ½ a leek (I always use the green tops as I don't cook with these), 2 celery sticks (the

heart and the leaves have loads of flavour), 1 onion and a few herbs. However, it is not an exact science and the more vegetables you add, the better your stock will taste.

By no means do you have to use your best veg for this. Making is stock is a very economical and sensible way of using up bits that perhaps have seen better days, so bear this in mind when looking for a way to use up neglected vegetables.

Cover completely with cold water and put onto the hob. Bring to the boil and simmer your stock, covered, on a very low heat for 4–6 hours.

Skim the top, using a ladle, as the impurities start to be released from the bones.

Top the stock up with water if it is boiling away at all. It is important to keep everything covered at all times.

Once you are happy with the flavour of your stock remove the pan from the heat and allow to cool before straining into a large container and placing into the fridge. The bones and vegetables have now done their job and can be thrown away.

Once the stock is cold, you may notice that a layer of fat has formed on the top. This needs to be scraped off and discarded. I would now freeze half, ready for my Sunday lunch gravy and leave the other half in the fridge, ready to use for a midweek risotto. **For a vegetable stock prepare as above omitting the chicken bones.**

Gravy

Chicken Gravy
1 tablespoon plain flour
175ml white wine
600ml chicken stock (see stock above)
1½ tablespoons redcurrant jelly

While your roast chicken is resting, you can make your gravy. Remove the chicken from the roasting tin and place it on a board or serving platter. Remove the lemon and garlic, or anything else that you may have put into the cavity of your chicken to enhance the flavour. Place the roasting tin you cooked the chicken in on the hob on a low heat.

Drain off the fat that may be in the roasting pan, but leave the dark liquid and the roasting bits from the bottom of the pan. If you used garlic cloves when cooking the chicken, squeeze them from their skins into the tray. Add the flour and, using a wooden spoon, scrape any bits from the bottom of the roasting tin as these will add flavour to your gravy.

Next, pour in the white wine and chicken stock (see page above for a recipe but a liquid shop-bought or stock cube will also be fine). Allow the mixture to come to the boil, then simmer for 5–6 minutes to allow it

to thicken and cook the flour. Finally, add the redcurrant jelly for a lovely sweetness and leave to simmer for another 5 minutes or so while you carve your chicken. Serve the gravy in a warmed gravy jug and drizzle generously over roast chicken.

For a lamb or beef gravy, follow the instructions above and substitute the following ingredients:
1 tablespoon plain flour
175ml red wine
600ml lamb or beef stock
1½ tablespoons redcurrant jelly

Index